THE ROLE OF AFRICA IN
THE CLOSING PHASE
OF HUMAN HISTORY

ABOUT THE AUTHOR

Charles Columbus King, born in Jacksonville, Florida, and reared in the southern United States of America, has spent most of his sixty-four years of life in humanitarian endeavors. Graduated from Claflin College, Orangeburg, South Carolina, Magna Cum Laude, 1938, with an A.B. degree in sociology, he enrolled the same year at the School of Religion, Howard University, Washington, D.C. Three years later, an honor graduate, he went on to The Divinity School, The University of Chicago, pursuing studies leading toward the Ph.D. degree. While enrolled there he taught Old Testament courses at the School of Religion, Howard University, including the Hebrew language and grammar, a basic tool of biblical exegesis. After four years in this academic context, he felt the irresistible urge to return to the pastorate from which he had been preempted. He has served from that vantage point ever since (1947). Always manifesting a deep interest in the downtrodden and disadvantaged, the Rev. Mr. King has maintained himself and a family of four in a variety of occupations which include industrial technician, janitor, carpenter, cement worker, social work administrator, painter, taxicab driver, and a few more. He said that the present book is in response to a divine mandate (revelation and assignment) outflowering from his many years on the crossroads of life.

THE ROLE OF AFRICA IN THE CLOSING PHASE OF HUMAN HISTORY

(A REVELATION)

By

CHARLES C. KING

THE CHRISTOPHER PUBLISHING HOUSE
WEST HANOVER, MASSACHUSETTS
02339

COPYRIGHT © 1981
BY CHARLES C. KING

Library of Congress Catalog Card Number 81-51735

ISBN: 0-8158—0406—7

All Rights Reserved

This book must not be sold. Anyone doing so will be under the curse of God, The Almighty One.

No portion of this book may be reproduced in print without the written permission of the author in advance. All radio and television rights are reserved to the author and/or his legally authorized representatives.

PRINTED IN
THE UNITED STATES OF AMERICA

"... to God the Judge of all, and to the spirits of just men made perfect, and to Jesus the mediator of the new covenant..." *(Hebrews 12: 23-24)* this labor of love is reverently, solemnly, and obediently dedicated.

Charles C. King

FOREWORD

I have studied anthropology, but I am not an anthropologist. I have studied archeology, but I am not an archeologist. I have delved into philosophy and all manner of philosophical systems. I know my way around in all major and most minor ones, but I am not primarily a philosopher. I have a degree in religion, but I make no claim to being a systematic theologian. I have a degree in sociology, and minored, while pursuing it, in psychology; still my claim to fame is not as either a sociologist or a psychologist.

Then who or what am I? What do I represent and what do I espouse? On what platform do I speak? On what stage do I perform? What credentials do I bring to claim a right to ask your indulgence, to preempt your valued time even to listen to what I have to say?

I am a prophet of God. I say it without blinking or apology. Mind you, this is not a boast. For a boastful braggart is, by that very token, a bigot, a bully, and a bluff — a fake, a charlatan and a phony. Such an one should be discredited summarily, and his message and proposals rejected out of hand.

But what is a prophet of God? He is one who has been chosen by God to declare and disclose what God is in process of doing, what He is going to do, and to articulate the message of God in terms that are understandable by the ordinary John Does and Susie Coes in the marketplaces of society, on the crossroads of life. A prophet of God is one who is separated, dedicated, consecrated for that one role. It is not because he is better than other people. He is no whit better than the least on the lowest rungs of the ladder of humanity in its struggles. He is chosen of God because God has to break through and communicate precious truth to His creatures — truth that is vital to their survival and wellbeing — and He must start somewhere.

In His infinite wisdom God makes the choice of His spokesman, His agent, often to the amazing puzzlement of everyone; for God is utterly unpredictable, incalculable. The computers will always miss it where He is concerned, for He alone can program such a computer to succeed in such a project. And God does not build computers. He doesn't need them.

I reaffirm it: I am a prophet of God. Some fifteen to twenty years ago He disclosed to me certain things that are relevant to the present generation and are crucial to the future to which this generation looks with mixed feelings of hope and trepidation. Primarily the disclosure relates to the black and darker peoples of the world. Hence the subject of this dissertation: Africa's Role in the Closing Phase of Human History. I am not out to prove a point, spin out any argument. Rather, I am presenting to you the realities of a situation in which you, directly or indirectly, for better or for worse, are involved. This truth, made known abroad to humanity is destined to have a momentous impact upon Washington, D.C., the United States of America, and on all the nations on this planet.

I have no interest in persuading you, propagandizing nor pressuring you into joining a campaign or crusade. A movement growing out of the revelations I shall present will emerge and will not be contained nor stopped until the end of the present age. In fact, in its incipient stage, it has already begun. To you who manifest sufficient interest, curiosity and concern in the subject here discussed to read and ponder it, I will share a great revelation in the spirit of "to whom it may concern for what it may be worth." After that, the posture you assume, what attitude you take, is strictly your business.

CONTENTS

Preface	5
Introduction	11
Africa in Reference in the Bible	17
Deep Are the Roots	29
The Hidden Gold Mine and the Sleeping Giant	33
Africa's Unique Role (The Black Horse)	41
Something in the Melting Pot That Won't Melt	59
The New World, America the Beautiful, The City Foursquare	87
The Conclusion of the Whole Matter	105

INTRODUCTION

As I take pen in hand this September 21, 1980, my environment provides a vivid contrast to the framework of mental thrust in anticipation of my preparing this manuscript for publication. I am seated on a log in an isolated spot along the bicycle trail in Rock Creek Park in Washington, D.C., U.S.A. The weather is a perfect fall day with mild sunshine. The fairly frequent passersby have a lively freewheeling gait and some a smile as I note their passing at a convenient distance for non-distraction. The birds sing and chirp cheerily. The familiar common insects of the out-of-doors satisfy their curiosity about an intruder but stay a distance that poses no threat to me nor them. Even they are friendly and courteous.

Yet I am preoccupied with cogitations that have to do with the closing phase of human history. What a contrast! But I must declare the revelation. It is a mandate from God. The starting point is an experience I had upwards of fifteen years ago while systematically reading and meditating upon the book of Revelation in my (the Christian) Bible. I had many times read passages from this book; a few times I had read it through, with considerable understanding. My mind, well trained in biblical exegesis and New Testament history, even higher and lower criticism, had served me about as well as these disciplines were designed to do. Having studied the original languages of scripture, Greek and Hebrew (having taught the language and grammar of the latter in the university), and, having come to the study of these from a fairly good grounding in Latin, I felt a sense of competency and at-homeness in getting down to what seemed to me the basic truths of this last book in the canon of Christian scripture.

Surprise of surprises, however, this particular time, a distinctly different mood enveloped and possessed me as I got beyond the introductory statement of the author, the beloved Apostle John. It seemed he must have been with me at the scene of my study and had decided to enlighten me as to the deeper meaning of significant passages and symbolism I had touched at a lighter level. I realized more than ever before how one can read the word of God, even seriously meditate upon it, and yet not dredge out the precious ore or mine the rare gems that are there. An angel had been given the task of unfolding the original revelation to John on the "isle that is called Patmos": "And I John saw these things, and heard them. And when I had heard and seen, I fell down to worship before the feet of the angel which showed me these things. Then said he unto me, See thou do it not: for I am thy fellow-servant, and of thy brethren the prophets, and of them which keep the sayings of this book: worship God" (Rev. 22:8-9). I am not aware of the presence of an angel when my enlightenment came. However, I am sure that the insights that flooded both my intellect and my inner being were conveyed by the Holy Spirit. I am eternally thankful to Him.

Having gained this precious insight that made some of the most puzzling passages of Revelation crystal clear, what was I to do? So much of what I came to know, no one, to my knowledge, had come forward with before.

Well, I did nothing. For years I simply savored it and kept it under wraps. Then, one night in regular Bible study in the church I am pastoring, someone raised a question that evoked an answer that got me involved in a partial disclosure of "the hidden knowledge." You see, our church is nondenominational, so I feel no compulsion to restrict my interpretation of the scriptures to what is "officially approved"—no necessity for an organizational imprimatur, no "nihil obstat" stamp. I had long before become accustomed to an in-depth treatment of the subject matter in teaching of the Bible.

Once the genie was out of the bottle, and as other related questions were propounded, I felt compulsion, from intellectual integrity and spiritual responsibility for my flock, to give at least the essentials of the newly acquired insights into the meaning of this very important book that rings down the curtain on Biblical scriptures. My students were very regular in attendance and very earnest in seeking truth. There was no need for hesitation or reserve. So I gave it to them—in the full. Of course they were amazed but digested it, I judge, very well.

Now that the faithful knew, what next? I thought, and thought, and thought some more. Then it occurred to me, purely from rational considerations, that if the insights I had received were real and the interpretation I had made was accurate, somebody somewhere (other than myself) would come forward with coincident material. Furthermore, the events which had future relevance would unfold. So, again, I did nothing—but wait.

I waited for the greater part of twelve years for someone to take up the cudgels and, in the light of the revelation, make known to the world what the closing phase of human history would entail in terms of what the four horses in chapter six of Revelation really signify. I listened to sermons and expositions of this chapter on radio and television, but none clearly explained this mysterious symbolism. None came up with anything near what the black horse was meant to convey.

Occasionally someone would match what I had received in reference to the red horse and more frequently the pale horse.

Then, one day, while I was reading through my little book of original poems and meditations called "The Soul Delight" (Christopher Publishing House, Boston, Mass., 1961), I came to a poem that sprang to new life as I read it once more:

> It might be when you're disconcerted
> When others fail the great tasks to do,
> 'Tis the voice of God that whispers low:
> "After all, it's up to you."

That triggered it. I had the same sort of feeling as when I was first blessed with the revelation. The Holy Spirit said, "Why do you wait? Don't you realize that nobody else is going to come forward with it because they don't have it. That is why I blessed YOU with it. It's YOUR job. Now, get going. The time is so short. Drop everything else and declare from the housetops what I have whispered in your ear." I had no choice but to obey.

To do so would necessitate some radical changes in the pattern of my life. For one thing, I would need to set up a series of public meetings for the purpose of disseminating the information. Also I would have to do this at the national capitol about which so much of the material in the revelation centered. Then I would have to take leave from the church I am pastoring long enough and at frequent enough intervals to do the needed work in Washington, D.C. and still keep continuity with the work being carried on by the church in Jacksonville, Florida.

In an official church meeting September 14, 1980, at 4:00 p.m., I requested approximately three weeks leave to go to Washington and begin pursuing the matter. My request was granted and my round-trip bus fare allocated. On Wednesday, September 17, at 6:30 p.m., I boarded the bus with all members present to see me off and praying for me. I arrived in Washington, D.C. next morning at 9:15.

The Lord had directed me a couple of weeks before to find a room and lodge in Seat Pleasant, Maryland, a little town in the suburbs of Washington. I did, and in a few days settled down to writing this book which contains all the important things disclosed to me concerning the sixth chapter of Revelation.

Chapter One

AFRICA IN REFERENCE IN THE BIBLE

AFRICA, MORE SPECIFICALLY, ETHIOPIA, IS MENTIONED IN THE ACCOUNT OF THE CREATION OF THE WORLD. In chapter two of Genesis, the first book of the Bible, the following occurs: "And there went up a mist from the earth, and watered the whole face of the ground. And the Lord God formed man of the dust of the ground, and breathed into his nostrils the breath of life; and man became a living soul. And the Lord God planted a garden eastward in Eden; and there he put the man whom he had formed. And out of the ground made the Lord God to grow every tree that is pleasant to the sight and good for food; the tree of life also in the midst of the garden, and the tree of knowledge of good and evil. And a river went out of Eden to water the garden; and from thence it was parted, and became four heads. The name of the first is Pison: that is it which compasseth the whole land of Havilah, where there is gold; and the gold of that land is good: there is the bdellium and the onyx stone. And the name of the second river is Gihon: the same is it that compasseth THE WHOLE LAND OF ETHIOPIA. And the name of the third river is Hiddekel: that is it which goeth toward the east of Assyria. And the fourth river is Euphrates" (Gen. 2:6-14).

The only river which compasseth (surrounds) the whole land of Ethiopia is the Nile, which is in Africa from beginning to end. It originates in the high-plateau region, and flows down to Egypt and empties into the Mediterranean Sea. The Hebrew word, and Old Testament name for Ethiopia is "Cush." It appears in the same form throughout the Old Testament. It is NOT CONTROVERSIAL. Ethiopia is the only country named in the story of creation which still bears the same precise name today. In all reasonable likelihood, it is the only country on the face of the whole earth which will bear the same name from the beginning of the world to its end. This is no accident, but fits into the Divine Providence. It is most remarkable that Ethiopia is the sole nation that has retained its national identity through every generation of mankind according to BIBLICAL DOCUMENTATION. Ethiopia has been identified with the black race throughout history. Let it be said now that those apologists who blush and blink at that fact when they come to the references in the Bible, and then invent theories that tend to unauthenticate the Biblical references to the black nation, are as far off from reality as the east is from the west. I have carefully examined all the speculative presentments by theologians and anthropologists that try to identify non-African, non-black peoples as the Ethiopians of Bible reference. They are all bankrupt. Biblical sources themselves provide the most authentic context for establishing the validity of its own usage.

Let us take, for example, an incident right from the pages of the Bible, which has been deliberately and most discreetly played down by most and suppressed by many Bible teachers, pastors, and other interpreters of scripture. I refer to the marriage of Moses, the great emancipator of the Hebrews (ancestors of the Jews) and establisher of the nation of

Israel. Just pick up a Bible and read the twelfth chapter of Numbers. The whole chapter is devoted to the circumstances including and following upon Moses's marriage. It begins: "And Miriam and Aaron spake against Moses because of the Ethiopian woman whom he had married: for he had married an Ethiopian woman" (Numbers 12:1). Note that the furor that followed was caused by Moses's immediate family—led by his sister and brother. What could be more normal and natural. Note further that they tried to justify their objections to this unquestionably interracial marriage by buttressing their prejudices with divine sanctions. This type of subterfuge is a basic weakness in human nature and will manifest in social situations and human relations to the end of time.

The vehemence with which they protested was prompted by the contrasts which the situation presented: Moses had stepped outside of his race in choosing a marriage partner. This usually brings objections by groups on both sides, but especially from the dominant group.

Miriam and Aaron laid their claim to the right to pass judgment on the situation because of their own interpretation of their religious experiences: "And they said, Hath the Lord indeed spoken only by Moses? hath he not spoken also by us?" (Numbers 12:2). Our religious experiences are subjective, therefore with a substantial emotional content, usually enshrouded in our pet prejudices. That is why we need more than our experiences to establish basic truth and insure the true will of God to be operative in our lives. We need the word—every word—of God. James the Apostle warned against this kind of subjective approach to God-ordained wisdom: "Who is a wise man and endued with knowledge among you? Let him show out of a good conversation his works with meekness of wisdom. But if ye have bitter envying and strife in your hearts, glory not, and lie not against the truth. This wisdom descendeth not from above, but is earthy, sensual, devilish. For where envying and strife is, there is confusion and every evil work. But the wisdom that is from above is first pure, then peaceable, gentle, and easy to be entreated, full of mercy and good fruits, without partiality, and without hypocrisy. And the fruit of righteousness is sown in peace of them that make peace" (James 3:13-18). Miriam and Aaron (according to the record) did not ask of God before they protested but merely assumed and jumped to conclusions and rested upon tradition. And swift punishment came from God. Now Numbers is the fourth book in the Bible. And this incident was in the formative stages of the nation of Israel. Moses and his black wife Zipporah had children. This black strain continued, therefore to manifest in the nation.

Notice that Miriam and Aaron had exactly the same approach which cropped up in the garden of Eden when the devil sought to derail Adam and Eve: "And he said unto the woman, Yea, hath God said Ye shall not eat of every tree of the Garden?" (Genesis 3:1). What is subtle in both instances is that by inference they were discrediting Divine credentials. Satan's approaches and human nature do not change. Jesus once answered a group of Pharisees who questioned the rightness of His actions by saying to them: "Why do ye also transgress the commandment of God by your tradition? . . . Thus have ye made the commandment of God of non-effect by your tradition. Ye hypocrites, . . . teaching for doctrines the commandments of men" (St. Matthew 15:3, 6b, 7, 9).

The word — every word — must be the final determinant. Thus you find Miriam's and Aaron's objections discredited and their attitude rebuked: "And the Lord heard it" (Numbers 12:2b). The Lord punished Miriam, the obvious instigator, and Aaron (guilty, as in the case of the golden calf episode, of complicity by yielding under pressure to what he knew in his heart was contrary to the will of God and His word). The journey to the promised land was held up for a week because of the protest by the family when Moses married an Ethiopian woman.

But, you may say, you still haven't proved that she was black, or African. To this I reply with a question: Where was Moses when he chose this woman for his wife? HE WAS IN AFRICA! The Sinai, where Moses spent forty years before he delivered the Hebrews from Egyptian slavery, is in Africa. Look it up on your map. Jethro, the priest who gave Moses the wife, and who taught Moses some basic principles of organization and administration when Moses came back there with the people (See Exodus 18:13-27), was a native African in Africa.

Take another example. In Jeremiah's prophecy a reference is made, at a point, to the unchanging association of a black skin with the Ethiopian: "Can the Ethiopian change his skin, or the leopard his spots?" (Jeremiah 13:23). To say (in the Bible) that a person was Ethiopian was tantamount to saying he was of black skin.

Although Biblical references to Africa are not abundant, they are well distributed. During the time when Israel was a kingdom, there were times when she found herself in active relationship with Ethiopia. Sometimes it was peaceful, sometimes otherwise. During one of the darkest hours of Judah's history when Hezekiah was king and Isaiah the prophet was his close advisor, one Tirhakah is mentioned in conjunction with the serious international crisis that threatened Judah's survival: "So Rab-shakeh returned and found the king of Assyria warring against Libnah: for he had heard that he was departed from Lachish. And when he heard say of Tirhakah king of Ethiopia, Behold he is come out to fight against thee: he sent messengers again to Hezekiah . . ." (II Kings 19:8-9). This Tirhakah must have commanded a pretty strong military force to dare to challenge that of the great Assyrian Empire which was at that time the scourge of the nations.

During the time of the united kingdom of Israel when Solomon reigned, the Queen of Sheba paid him a visit, asking him hard questions and presenting him with expensive gifts (I Kings 10: 1-10; II Chron. 9:1-12). According to tradition, this black Queen of Ethiopia became the mother of a child fathered by King Solomon. Now at that time, Ethiopia's extensive empire included the territory then known as Nubia (or the Sudan). Several designations of this region are found in the records: there is of course Cush. And there is also Axoum. Then there is also Negus (referring to the rulers who took this title: "King of kings"). There persisted a legend in the territory that King Solomon and the Queen of Sheba contributed to the line of rulers.

The account of the Queen's visit to Solomon as it occurs in II Chronicles (9:12) ends on a note that tends to corroborate the legend: "And King Solomon gave to the Queen of Sheba all her desire, whatsoever she asked, beside that which she had brought unto the king. So she turned and went away to her own land, she and her servants."

The prophet Jeremiah lived and prophesied during the twilight of Judah's kingdom. He witnessed the enslavement of the Jews by Nebuchadnezzar, king of the Babylonian Empire. Jeremiah was known as both "the weeping prophet" and "the prophet of doom and gloom." He was much disliked and persecuted by high officials and religious leaders alike. Once he was thrown into a dungeon and left to perish as he sank deep in soft mud. But through the providence of the God in whose name he declared his messages and the compassion of an Ethiopian citizen of Judah who learned of his fate, the prophet was rescued. Jeremiah tells of the experience in chapter thirty-eight of that book that bears his name: "Therefore the princes said unto the king, we beseech thee let this man be put to death: for thus he weakeneth the hands of the men of war that remain in this city, and the hands of all the people, in speaking such words unto them: for this man seeketh not the welfare of this people, but the hurt. Then Zedekiah the king said, Behold he is in your hand, for the king is not he that can do anything against you. Then took they Jeremiah and cast him into the dungeon of Malchiah the son of Hammelech, that was in the court of the prison: and they let down Jeremiah with cords. And in the dungeon there was no water, but mire: so Jeremiah sank in the mire. Now when Ebed-melech the Ethiopian, one of the eunuchs which was in the king's house, heard that they had put Jeremiah in the dungeon, the king then sitting in the gate of Benjamin, Ebed-melech went forth out of the king's house, and spake to the king, saying, My Lord the king, these men have done evil in all that they have done to Jeremiah the prophet, whom they have cast into the dungeon, and he is like to die from hunger in the place where he is: for there is no more bread in the city. Then the king commanded Ebed-melech the Ethiopian, saying, take from hence thirty men with thee, and take up Jeremiah the prophet out of the dungeon, before he die. So Ebed-melech took the men with him, and went into the house of the king under the treasury, and took thence old cast clouts and old rotten rags, and let them down by cords into the dungeon to Jeremiah. And Ebed-melech said unto Jeremiah, Put now these old cast clouts and rotten rags under thine armholes under the cords. And Jeremiah did so. So they drew up Jeremiah with cords, and took him up out of the dungeon: and Jeremiah remained in the court of the prison. Then Zedekiah the king sent and took Jeremiah the prophet unto him into the third entry that is in the house of the Lord..." (Jer. 38:4-14).

Ezekiel the prophet makes mention of Ethiopia in forecasting the events of the last days before the coming of the Messiah and the restoration of Israel to a golden age. In designating the nations that will be on the side of "the northern army" (Russia) that will invade Israel, Ezekiel includes Ethiopia (Ezek. 38: 5). Most astute prediction in the light of contemporary political developments in Ethiopia: recently gone over to a Communist government after being a Christian nation from the time of the Apostles.

Daniel, the prophet during the time of the exile of the Jews in Babylon, in veiled symbolism (which we shall deal with specifically in a subsequent chapter), predicts the rise of Africa to world prominence at the approaching end of the age (Dan. 7:6).

Perhaps one of the most famous and significant developments in reference to Ethiopia in the Bible is that recorded in the eighth chapter of the book of The Acts of the Apostles: "And the angel of the Lord spake unto Philip, saying, Arise, and go toward the south unto the way that goeth down from Jerusalem to Gaza, which is desert. And he arose and went: and, behold, a man of Ethiopia, an eunuch of great authority under Candace queen of the Ethiopians, who had the charge of all her treasure, and had come to Jerusalem for to worship, was returning, and sitting in his chariot read Esaias the prophet. Then the Spirit said unto Philip, Go near, and join thyself to this chariot. And Philip ran thither to him, and heard him read the prophet Esaias, and said, Understandest thou what thou readest? And he said, How can I, except some man should guide me? And he desired Philip that he would come up and sit with him. The place of the scripture where he read was this, He was led as a sheep to the slaughter; and like a lamb dumb before his shearer, so opened he not his mouth: in his humiliation his judgment was taken away:

and who shall declare his generation? for his life is taken from the earth. And the eunuch answered Philip, and said, I pray thee, of whom speaketh the prophet this? of himself or of some other man? Then Philip opened his mouth, and began at the same scripture, and preached unto him Jesus. And as they went on their way they came unto a certain water: and the eunuch said, See, here is water, what doth hinder me to be baptized? And Philip said, If thou believest with all thine heart, thou mayest. And he answered and said, I believe that Jesus Christ is the Son of God. And he commanded the chariot to stand still: and they went down both into the water, both Philip and the Eunuch; and he baptized him. And when they were come up out of the water, the Spirit of the Lord caught away Philip, that the eunuch saw him no more: and he went on his way rejoicing" (Acts 8:26-39). Several things are worthy of special attention here.

First, note that the chariot was going down from Jerusalem. Philip was directed by the Spirit to go down. The man was returning to Africa.

Next, note that the Ethiopian had been to Jerusalem to WORSHIP. He had to be familiar with the religion of the Jews in order to participate in their worship. No doubt he was one of the many proselites referred to in Acts: "And there were dwelling at Jerusalem Jews, devout men, out of every nation under heaven" (Acts 2:5). This Ethiopian eunuch might well have been one of those who made the annual pilgrimage and might have been there at the great Pentecost celebration.

Next, please note that this man was reading the scriptures in Isaiah (Esaias) which was written in Hebrew. He had to have knowledge of that language.

Next, note that Philip, perceiving the man to be a foreigner, probably addressed him in Greek, the universal language of that day. The fact that he replied to Philip would suggest that the Ethiopian spoke Greek. One thing is certain, Philip did not speak the eunuch's native language. The man was a very top government official and was of surpassing intelligence and culture.

Last of all, note that Christianity was introduced into Ethiopia during the days of the Apostles, in the very first century A.D. It was introduced through the direct preaching of a deacon in the first church, so it must have been the pure, unadulterated, authentic "faith once delivered to the saints" (Jude 3). This should be a sobering fact to so many modern Christians of European and American vintage who seem to think that the Christianizing of the African was a task begun by their missionary efforts over a thousand years later. While most of Europe was still worshiping pagan gods, Christ was well known in the heart of Africa. The white Christians are now trying to Christianize Africans in places where they long ago brutally dehumanized them through the slave trade and demoralized them through commercial exploitation. Even while I am writing this, the process is not abated altogether in parts of Africa, notably Rhodesia and South Africa.

In the book of Acts at another point a significant though brief reference is made to another black man: "Now there were in the church that was at Antioch certain prophets and teachers; as Barnabas, and Simeon that was called Niger, and Lucius of Cyrene, and Manaen, which had been brought up with Herod the Tetrarch, and Saul. And as they ministered to the Lord, and fasted, the Holy Ghost said, Separate me Barnabas and Saul for the work whereunto I have called them. And when they had fasted and prayed, and laid their hands on them, they sent them away" (Acts 13:1-3).

Let us note here that Simeon was without doubt a black

man, for the term by which he was distinguished from the others in this group means "black" (the latin word used here). Hence, Simeon called black, or "the black one." This man is said to have been in the church at Antioch a prophet and/or a teacher. He could have been either or both according to the context. Antioch was where the disciples were first called Christians. This suggests that at a very early stage in the Apostolic Church, blacks were an integral part. Saul of Tarsus, later became the great evangelist (maybe the greatest). Paul, the Apostle who wrote most of the New Testament, was launched on his great missionary career with the hands of this black man upon him.

In Revelation, chapter six, there occurs a bit of symbolism which brings Africa into reference in a strategic role in the windup of the present historical process. I refer to the third of the four horses: the BLACK horse. I shall have much to say about this in another chapter. Suffice it to say here that the horse is distinctly black, in contrast to the others, and the rider of this horse is the only one who holds a peaceful instrument.

There are other references to Africa in the scriptures—enough to convince anyone with an open mind—that Africa has played a prominent part in the biblical drama on the stage of human history. We list a few more without comment: Esther 1:1; Job 28:19; Ps. 68:31; 87:4; Isaiah 11:11; 18:1; 20:3; 20:5; 43:3; 45:14; Jer. 39:15-18; Ezekiel 29:10, 30: 4, 5, 9; II Chron. 12:3; 14:9, 12, 13; 16:8; 21:16; Daniel 11:43; Amos 9:7; Nahum 3:9; Zephaniah 2:12; 3:10.

Chapter Two

DEEP ARE THE ROOTS

If the entire geographical configuration were visualized as a giant tree, Africa would most appropriately figure as the root system. The first stirrings of growth, antedating trunk, limbs, leaves, and fruit are the roots, and the subsequent stability of the whole organism depends upon the fabric.

More and more the search for origins is turning to Africa, not designedly so much as of necessity. In seeking to correct the margin of error in their own researches and conclusions, the more persistent scholars in anthropology, archeology, and geology have had to follow trails that lead to Africa. Less than a century ago, any suggestion that a search should be launched on the African continent for the origin of the human race or the cradle of civilization would have been treated (in western circles) with impatience, if not with outright contempt. Yet, today, this very trend, unsuggested, has developed from random and accidental discoveries.

"Primitive" has gained a new connotation in the so-called civilized mind. The term can be taken more nearly literally as one views the exhibits of sculpture, painting, and the various crafts in the sophisticated salons where once these products of the African culture were disqualified or relegated to mostly out-of-the-way backdrops. African models are being sought after because of the grace and elegance which their native cultures normally designed them for in the pursuit of normal everyday interests. The burdens atop their heads promoted balance not only of the load but also of the human frame in locomotion. They do not need to pay expensive fees and attend schools to "finish" them for the art. Strange how for so many centuries westerners put books and other objects upon their heads and "practiced" the same essentials as the "savage" while at the same time looking upon his real cousin in nature with disdain.

Currently the world of music is being transformed by a turning to the basic patterns of rhythm and tonality which for thousands of years have been in vogue on "the dark continent." Whether one goes to the discotheque, the jazz festival, the gospel sing, or the Boston Pops concert, there is that constant strain, that haunting refrain which one can trace unmistakably to Africa. In Latin America and the Caribbean it is pronounced, due to the influx of African slaves. So long did the whites ridicule it, then ignore it, then tolerate it, then plagiarize it, then open the front door and ADOPT it — without benefit of proper legal procedures or cultural identification and recognition. I have actually been in circles where white people innocently and naively thought that gospel music was originated by hillbillies and sort of "taken over" by blacks, an absurdity which the humblest blacks recognize as such.

The sculptured works from native African hands and concepts are more and more winning a place — their rightful place — of real respectability in art centers around the world. The same holds true of the dance. Highly industrialized societies, through their corporations' researches, have found that the first developments and significant strides in metallurgy are traceable to the natives of southern Africa. Archeologists are corroborating the stories handed down by word-of-mouth tribal tradition that their African ancestors taught the world to work with copper and iron.

Yes, even in the all important department of human endeavor, religion, Africa stands out. Lost in the distant past are the beginnings of the monotheistic concept, far antedating the Israelite thrust. Long before Moses led the Hebrews out of Egyptian slavery, the Egyptians were building temples and practicing rituals to worship one god to whom they attributed all origins and destiny. The pyramids are still mute testimony to their credo. It (the pyramid) has found a place on the American dollar. Let it not be forgotten, although many never learned it, that Egypt is in Africa. Moses led the Hebrews out of Africa to the promised land.

At a meeting of the world's most prominent anthropologists in very recent years, there was almost unanimous agreement that the origin of the human race was in Africa and that somewhere between there and China, but not the fertile crescent, was the dawn of human civilization. The closing phase and the opening phase of culture may yet experience a "family reunion" with a common geneology. The family home, Africa, will probably provide the setting.

Chapter Three

THE HIDDEN GOLD MINE
AND THE SLEEPING GIANT

EVER SINCE THE RISE OF WESTERN CIVILIZATION, AFRICA HAS BEEN AT ONCE A GOLD MINE AND A SLEEPING GIANT. She was more or less ingrown. The natural geographical situation encouraged such a status. So much of the coastline is unsuitable for port facilities that the African nations never developed maritime pursuits to any great extent. Sandbars sort of hemmed them in. To be sure, inland trade routes were well established from the ancient days of the Pharaohs, and her merchants found world markets in some centers of international intercourse, mainly in the Middle East where a land bridge connected the three continents. With natural resources in abundance — rivers teeming with fish, forests and fields flushed with flocks and herds in the wild, birds of every conceivable variety, rich lands easily cultivable — the native African had, like the American Indian, little incentive to adventure off into far-off unknown regions. It was a marked contrast to the Western European nations whose pressing need for resources to support the demands of an ever-increasing competitive style of life forced them to go far beyond their own boundaries in search. Compared with other regions of the world, with comparable resources, however, Africa remained relatively let-alone and unexplored. Her northern border on the Mediterranean Sea promoted interesting and quite active relations with the seafaring nations of southern Europe—Spain, Portugal, Italy, Greece—from ancient times. But all this was like a layer or crust, a cap upon the head while the body remained unclad and unadorned.

It was not until modern times that this great reservoir of resources was "discovered" and exploited. The trend to industrialization in the western world, stimulated and spurred on by the inventive genius of the men of science, brought about a great need and search for raw materials to nurture the growing appetite of another giant, namely, mass production industry. As the appetite became insatiable, the nations on the vanguard of this new industrialization—England, Germany, France, Italy, Spain—sent their mariners everywhere to procure the raw materials that were elevating the standard of living of an ever-broadening middle class at home. These materials came from many places around the world: China, India, the Americas, the islands of the Pacific; but the real treasure-trove of the age was Africa. So it was gobbled up by a handful of European nations, some very small, as in the case of Holland, Belgium, and Portugal (who got in on the act in time). Africa was literally staked out or colonized. Unlike the Americas, where the European explorers settled and developed on-the-scene old-country cultures, Africa was regarded more as a victim is regarded by a predatory beast: as a means of satiating a present-felt hunger. And, also like the predator, these nations were content to simply guard and guarantee supply from their individual territories. Notable exceptions were the English and the Dutch who made permanent settlements in South Africa, literally transplanting their own culture intact in the midst of what they regarded as a vast howling wilderness amid

Closing Phase of Human History

primitive savages hardly worthy of the designation of human. The indigenous population were treated exactly as the other objects of interest, viz., raw materials. And thus, their principal resource, their labor, was utilized much in the same way that one with profits and trade in view, hews down trees or plows the earth for mineral ore. The human resources were to all intents and purposes natural resources to be treated as such. The question of human rights applied only to white settlers. To the native stock it was an irrelevancy.

In addition to the merchandise of various raw materials that this land of Africa provided, there was a great bonus: the merchandise of the abundant resource of natives to serve as free labor on the plantations of the Europeans who had transplanted their culture to and were making their homes in the Americas. Slave trading became the companion commerce of dealings in timber, gold, diamonds, ivory, mahogany, spices, etc. It was regarded in exactly the same way by the entrepreneur. The human aspect was negligible and purely incidental. For over a hundred years whole organized corporations plied the slave TRADE and built up a peculiar segment in the population of the New World, a segment which, after their eventual emancipation, would haunt their "fellow citizens" as did Banquo's ghost in Shakespeare's Hamlet.

Africa not only will play a crucial role in the closing phase of human history, but it has been a decisive factor in the shaping of the world into what it is today. The world convulsed twice in a lifetime in terms of World Wars One and Two, the latter of which instigated the introduction of atomic weapons that have constituted the single most critical factor in international relations ever since. The real cause of World War One was the contest among the industrialized nations of Europe for the raw resources which the colonial possessions (mainly in Africa) yielded. All other causes are subsidiary. Like the dogs over the proverbial bone, the nations of Europe scrapped.

When the victorious Allied Powers dictated the terms of the peace, the vanquished Central Powers, led primarily by Germany, were stripped of their colonial possessions, and thus deprived of the very lifeblood of their economies. Automatically the seeds of World War Two were sown in soil fertilized by the blood and pride of a wounded and humiliated competitor in the industrial arena. Germany, as soon as she could regroup her forces and recoup from the shambles what losses were salvageable, came knocking loudly at the doors of the former Allied Powers to avenge her defeat, retrieve her honor, and regain her lost colonial possessions. Under the Nazi movement the German nation targeted and defeated one after another of her former enemies until bogged down and hindered by circumstances which only the hand of a Benign Providence could create and control. So World War Two was really phase two of World War One. The latter phase ended pretty much as had the first, with a crushing defeat of Germany, et al. But this time Germany wisened up. She turned smart. It is only a fool who neither learns nor profits by his misfortunes. This time Germany abandoned the military approach to retrieving what she had lost in terms of materials and the respect of the civilized world. She made a critical decision to pick up the pieces and, accepting the help of a former principal enemy, namely the United States of America, she set out to rebuild a great industrial economy that would rival the best and eclipse the lesser of her competitors. Today, a realistic appraisal of the international industrial situation will readily reveal that Germany has a success story which only Japan, another defeated foe (incidentally using the same approach) can match. As much as I would like to pursue this line of observation further, I must refrain from doing so by the necessity of getting down to the main subject of this dissertation. Suffice it to say here that a good look at the hard evidence of the effect of German (and Japanese) advance upon the American economy alone forces one to reconsider the question and to draw new conclusions as to who really won the war. Maybe "the pen is mightier than the sword" after all. I do not think that the German predilection for bellicosity has diminished, however. But she has discovered a new route to her goal of world power. So far, it is working.

One of the results which none of the European nations (nor their American ally, for that matter) anticipated was the widescale emancipation of the former colonial peoples from their dependent status. The rising tide of independent nationalism in Africa since World War Two is one of the most amazing phenomena in the history of political science and government. Who would have dreamed at the outset of the Nazi threats — of Adolph Hitler's fanatical rabble rousing rantings—that the whole train of newly-emerged independent black nations would be wielding the de facto balance of power in international affairs at the windup? The coalition of so-called third world countries in caucus and vote in the United Nations has kept a stranglehold on the jugular veins of the so-called superpowers and threatens to sound the death knell for western power politics in the traditional signification of that term. I shall deal with this more particularly in a spiritual context in a subsequent chapter.

One more subject merits consideration at this point. It is that which concerns the relationship between Christian missions and the colonial era in Africa. For the nature of that relationship holds a significant portent for the future so far as Africa's role is concerned.

Christian missions in Africa (and Asia), however nobly conceived and/or charitably motivated, ran a course that is most regrettable. In the minds of most missionaries, the confusion as to the differential between culture and Christ was colossal. Christian morality was conceived and implemented in terms of a ruthless disregard for practically everything in the native culture as having any value. Whole institutions were swept out overnight, long-standing traditions discarded with little or no evaluation of their functional relevance to the indigenous culture. Concepts of dignity and worth were recast in a mould which made them conformable to standards imported from another culture. For example, the "heathen" were told how sinful it is to worship their ancestors by people who came from cultures (still maintaining close family ties) where it was the norm to stage elaborate funerals and to build great memorials to perpetuate the memory of dead relatives. Even the sanctuaries of worship, in many cases, were punctuated with memorial windows, pews, organs, etc., that bore plates, sometimes quite ornate, with the names and virtues of the departed relatives. The practice of going periodically to the gravesites of loved ones departed and laying a floral bouquet upon their remains was in more cases than otherwise in vogue back in the missionaries' homeland. The semi-nude bodies of those to whom salvation was brought were forced to bear complete covering in utter disregard of the functional significance they bore to a tropical or subtropical climate. At the same time back at the missionaries' homeland, styles of dress played up sensuality and called attention to aspects of a sexual nature in a manner that gave the missionaries' teachings on dress a rather hollow ring. While the missionaries were mouthing and requiring rote memorizing of such preachments as "God is no respecter of persons" and "All are one in Christ Jesus," the fact of enforced segregation on a racial basis right within the mission station belied what was taught.

Once the missionaries had succeeded, deliberately or inadvertently, in convincing the natives that practically everything of value was imported from a foreign (Caucasian) culture, and, by implication, that almost nothing in the natives' system was bound to be honored, it was easy for the merchant to come in and superimpose his system of commercial values on that of the native population.

Soft drinks (in some cases hard), tobacco, refined sugar and its products, European-styled clothing (even top hats), etc., were plugged as "proper." Many things which came to be status symbols in the eyes and minds of the natives were no more than the deliberately-contrived trinkets and trappings of a foreign merchant to enrich his own coffers. Of course the missionaries themselves did not do this. But their silence and indifference while their fellow whites did amounted to de facto approval. Africa was commercially raped while the Christianizing efforts went on apace. It was like Saul of Tarsus looking on and guarding the coats of others of his kind while Stephen was stoned to death. He "was consenting" although not directly participating. The value system in economic exchange, regulated mainly by the foreigner, often left the natives with things they did not need while at the same time they yielded up things much needed but which were bought up and resold at an enormous profit. For money with which the natives bought the European's imported goods the natives sold things of high value, sometimes things of high nutritional value, which they should profit by. Without intending to do so, the missionaries softened up and conditioned native populations for economic exploitation by their white brothers. In time the true picture would be seen by the natives and a flood of objection and protest would surely follow. With the shedding of colonial shackles, the baby in many cases went down the drain with the wash water. The cause of Christian missions was aborted while the door was flung open to humanistic values and in some cases to outright antichristian Communism. To view the rising tide of communism and socialism among the independent nations of Africa apart from this unfortunate background of linkage between Christian missionary effort and the economically exploitive colonialism of pre-World War Two years is incredibly naive if not downright dishonest. No amount of decrying and denouncing of black nationals for accepting help from or embracing non-Christian sources in today's struggles for a place in the sun will roll back the tidal wave coming ever nearer our shores. Jeremiah the prophet once put it in the following terms when Judah was involved in an international crisis with the Babylonian Empire's army poised at the gates of Jerusalem: "If thou has run with the footmen, and they have wearied thee, then how canst thou contend with horses? And if in the land of peace, wherein thou trustedest, they wearied thee, then how wilt thou do in the swelling of Jordan? . . . I have forsaken mine house, I have left mine heritage, I have given the dearly beloved of my soul into the hand of her enemies" (Jer. 12:5, 7). Communism is, in my view, God's judgment upon an errant Christian witness, especially in foreign lands. "Christian foreign policy" has been bankrupt. And now, our only hope of redemptive solution is a reversal of the process. As ridiculous as this may sound, especially as it falls upon the ears of our white Christian brethren, it is my firm conviction that a great groundswell of indigenous Christian missionary zeal on the foreign (especially African) field must not only stem the tide of Communism in Africa, but must leap across the seas and not be spent until it has forced western white Christendom (including Christian democratic institutions) to face up to itself honestly, and in true repentance for its failings and hypocrisies of the past, cry out to God who sent our Savior to demonstrate His effectiveness to save a society as well as an individual soul. This is the closing phase of human history according to the Bible, and Africa, has a crucial role in it ACCORDING TO THE SCRIPTURES!

Chapter Four

AFRICA'S UNIQUE ROLE
(THE BLACK HORSE)

When one turns to the book of Revelation in the Bible, he is presented, through symbolic representations, with a comprehensive picture of the closing phase of human history as we have known it. The sure return of Jesus Christ to the earth to establish His (Father's) kingdom and reign over it for a thousand years is preceded by a sequence of developments that close out the present age or world system.

In the sixth chapter, there is presented a succession of four horses which brings us nearer and nearer the actual end. These are different in color. Their riders are equipped with certain instruments (except in the case of the fourth) which they hold in their hands and use in accordance with the purpose for which each was called forth. Each, in turn, accomplishes the specific task assigned to him by Divine Providence, then fades from the scene. This would make a nice children's story, but it was not written for children. It was put into the sacred scriptures for hard-headed, mature, CHRISTIAN adults. It is for Christ's servants. But alas, veiled as it is in symbols, who can unravel the mystery? Only God and those who, endued and imbued with His Holy Spirit, can really rightly divide the word that is there. Dear *rs*, I have been so privileged. All praise to God the mighty One, I hasten humbly to confess.

The general overall period of the end time encompassed there is from the rise of western (Greco-Roman) civilization to the end of the twentieth century. During this period there comes forth four major thrusts or movements of worldwide proportions. That is the significance of the four horses. They follow AFTER one another.

The white horse represents western civilization. It was nurtured and developed by white (Caucasian) peoples. Its center is in Europe, the home or native habitat of the white race. A cursory glance over the institutions of western culture will readily reveal their rootage in the Greek-Roman matrix. This point is too obvious to belabor. The white horse's appearance at this time signifies the world's domination by the white European nations for a given period. There comes on the historical scene for the first time an empire (the Greek) that is white (European). All the preceding ones had been Asiatic or African. This white horse should not be confused with another white horse that comes up in Revelation at a later point (Rev. 19:11). They are quite different in function and in the sequence unfolding the events of the last days. The empires of Alexander the Great and the Caesars of Rome extended themselves to the farthest reaches of the world then known on an organized basis. The conquest, at first military, was complete. Subjugated peoples were held in check by the military while a superimposition of the culture of the overlord governments blanketed those of the vanquished. Where Greece left off, geographically speaking, Rome took over and expanded until much of Asia and all of Europe were under one system — The Roman Empire.

This condition prevailed until, from internal disintegration by corruption, the barbarous tribesmen came down from northern and western Europe and caused the collapse of the Roman Empire in the fifth century A.D. It fell apart and a curious consequence ensued. The ecclesiastical arm of the empire, The Roman Catholic Church, took the necessary steps to become the power structure of the society. No longer by military means would Rome exert her influence. No longer would the Caesars sit at the pinnacle of state rule. No longer would the Senate function in laying down legal edicts. No longer would the Governors, Procurators, and other officials function in the same capacity in the Empire, keeping the peace and collecting the taxes in the outlying provinces. This all shifted to a new breed of Empire builders of ecclesiastical vintage. Under the guise of clerical vestments as purveyors of peace, the unsuspected neo-Roman Empire builders used the old framework to forward their expansive ambitions. They advanced the faith through indirect means of control — through the sovereigns who were loyal to the faith and through the enterprises of her merchants who received the blessings of the church as they prospered and enriched its coffers. It was a beautiful system. Hardly anyone questioned or challenged it. How could it fail? The Roman church had a virtual monopoly not only on the faith of Christian believers, but it held the subtle control of educational and economic institutions as well.

When in due course, the merchants of western Europe went around the world in search of bigger and better investments and more adequate resources with which to rebuild the empire's shattered economy, they went with the blessing of the Church of Rome and were in most cases accompanied by some of its clerical representatives. The principal explorers who brought Europe out of the throes of stagnation were Catholic. They went out as merchant mariners, but they also had a lively interest in propagating the Roman Catholic faith. It was a common practice for the priests who accompanied the merchants to establish missions among the peoples where the mariners' ships propelled them. The Roman Empire still functioned, but in a manner never dreamed of by the non-ecclesiastical hierarchy that sat at the helm of the ship-of-state before the fall of the Empire. To much farther regions than the old guard ever visualized or imagined, the Roman power spread like the green bay tree. Italian, Spanish, Portuguese, French, and Dutch explorers accomplished this with almost unchecked facility. Not until the English, under Protestant auspices, fought it out with their Catholic rivals and won the North American continent and certain portions of Asia was the process checked.

Please note the instrument that was given to the rider of the white horse before he rode forth on his mission. It was a bow (and, by inference, arrows). The arrow is a symbol of conquest. It is shot forth to cover DISTANCE. It goes ahead of the archer and subdues. Note that the stated purpose of the white horse was "to conquer." "And he went forth conquering." This is the story of the white man ever since the Greeks, under Alexander the Great, emerged from their relatively small habitat on the Aegean Sea of southern Europe to become the western world's first empire builders. The trend was started. Rome and England followed and achieved a galloping momentum. The white horse of European nationality complex rode around the world and conquered every continent on the globe—almost unchecked. The white man subjugated virtually all the peoples of the earth, either directly or indirectly, even the islands of the seas. He imposed his will and helped himself to the world's store of natural resources. He hauled them back to European ports from which they found their way into the fabric of a refined culture of opulence and affluence that built western civilization up to its zenith, which still remains to be eclipsed. The great banking houses, the business and industrial corporations blossomed and flourished. It seemed it would last forever.

Nevertheless, there is a Superpower that (Who) determines the destinies of nations. This is no less true of Ancient Assyria, Babylon, Persia, and Egypt than it is of modern Britain, France, Holland, Germany, Spain, Portugal, or Belgium. It is God, according to the scriptures, Who setteth up one and putteth down another. It is He who bringeth princes to naught. It is He who lifteth up the beggar from the trashpile and setteth him on high. This is no less applicable to nations than it is to individuals. World War One brought the passing of the sun over the sky's arched summit, commencing afternoon. World War Two brought western civilization to the hour of twilight. The closing phase of human history has begun.

The second horse, the red, is no longer waiting in the wings. God had released him and he has gone forth. He made his entry on the scene of history at the close of World War One. The red horse is Communism, and the rider spurred him into the main road at the Bolshevik Revolution that toppled the Czarist government of Russia. He has been overtaking the white horse at every turn: first in Europe, then in Asia, now in Africa, and is knocking at the gates of the Americas (mainly the southern continent).

Has it ever occurred to you that the Communists are, and have been from the beginning, associated with the red color? We refer to "red Russia" and "red China." But why? It is no accidental identification. The Bible, in Revelation, calls them red. The second (red) horse in the sixth chapter is Communism. This is the agent God has used to check the power of the white Caucasian power structure. Please note that the white Russian segment—extreme eastern Europe—

is negligible by comparison with the vast communist population that spans Asia, which has gone almost completely Communist. Vainly, the United States tried to stem the tide in Southeast Asia. The Viet Nam War was to all intents lost, an exercise in futility. Asia is destined to end up Communist just as surely as the Americas were to become Western European. A decade after the Viet Nam conflict, Southeast Asia is solidly under Communist domination. Now add Afghanistan. While I am writing this, the forces of Communism are being exerted in the Middle East in the armed conflict between Iran and Iraq.

Communism will never take firm root in America. It is for Asia. I will bring out in another chapter the reason why it will not succeed in America. It has definitely taken the control of the hitherto white-dominated world in Asia and parts of Africa. The black peoples of the world will never turn wholesale to the Communist banner, although a few nations will (according to Bible prophecy).

Consider the instrument (weapon) that was put into the hand of the rider of the red horse: "And there was given unto him a great sword" (Rev. 6:4). Unlike the bow and arrow, the sword is a weapon for close-up hand-to-hand combat. One wielding the sword has to get close to his enemy. This typifies the primary Communist strategy: subversion, infiltration, boring from within. The great sword was given for two purposes, viz., to "take peace from the earth" and "that they should kill one another." The peace of societies is upset by subversives at work in their midst. The peace of the world has been on tenterhooks ever since the Communist rise to power. And this inspite of SALT agreements, Detente, and the United Nations. None of these makes or will make any difference in checking the Communist disturbers of the peace. They will not only be checked but stopped. But this by the Divine Power only. The normal state of things Communist, judging by past performances, is for that red horse to take peace from the earth. The Communists will never negotiate anything in good faith. They are incapable of doing so. Whenever it appears that they do, it is an illusion. They will stall, evade, lie and deceive just long enough to maneuver into position to strike a timely strategic blow. Then watch out. The leopard will not change its spots, although he has learned the advantages of artful cosmetics. Communism has nothing to offer humanity but a sword—disruption of the peace and eventual mass destruction.

"That they should kill one another" is applicable to their ruthless methods of suppressing dissent and of maintaining their order of things. The rigors of forced hard labor and tortuous methods in mental institutions as imposed upon dissidents attest to this internal bloodletting propensity of the Communist mind. Mass purges such as were executed under Josef Stalin and Mao Tse Tung require little deliberation and virtually no adjudication in the process. They certainly conform to the mandate to "kill one another."

For those who are frightened at the advance of Communism in the world in one generation, take hope. The same God Who set the bounds of the sea, saying, "Thus far and no further," and "Thus shall ye proud waves be stayed," is the same Supreme Sovereign who sent the red horse across the stage of history and will stop him in his march when His (God's) purpose is accomplished. In the not-distant future we shall see the miraculous happen. The rug will suddenly be pulled out from under the Fidel Castros and all their ilk to the utter amazement of almost everyone, and their masters in the Kremlin will have their own hands so full that they won't be able to do what will be needed for their own schemes to continue to work.

Now we come to the next—the black—horse. You should be able to guess it by now: The black horse represents the black (and darker) peoples of the world, mainly African.

The first thing different that we note about the black horse is that its rider, unlike his predecessors, does not hold a WEAPON in his hand. There is a marked contrast. Instead of a weapon, the rider of the black horse has "a pair of balances in his hand" (Rev. 6:5). From the time of its invention the balance (scale) has been an instrument of peace, not war. It is used in the amicable transactions of the marketplace (not the battlefield) where men trade and bargain with one another IN GOOD FAITH. The person who is bent on conquering waives all considerations of right on the part of the objects of his conquests. The disturber of the peace relies upon his weapon to accomplish his aim. But the trader who consummates an ordinary peaceful transaction considers the (equal) value of that which his partner brings to the table. When men "shall beat their swords into plowshares and their spears into pruning hooks," when "nation shall not lift up sword against nation" nor occupy their minds with the study of military science and tactics anymore, when "they shall sit every man under his vine and fig tree and none shall make them afraid," the rider of the black horse will not have to make any changes. He will neither have to turn in his instrument nor undergo a psychological reorientation.

From the philosophical standpoint the balance has from ancient times been the symbol of fairness, justice and equity. It has been displayed as such in the courts. Thus, God has ordained by the circumstances of their situation down to the last days that the black peoples should be His instrument of justice. This role is reserved to them: to shore up things spiritually just before the return of the Lord Jesus Christ. The blacks are in a peculiar position to undertake this.

Closing Phase of Human History

Africa has been held down, held back, and exploited as no other people in modern times. Black peoples have a vivid and realistic background of experience for understanding and appreciating what real justice is. They have been denied it, have hungered and thirsted for it so long. They are more sensitive to human rights than any in all the world today. The rallying cry of the blacks through these modern times has been "Give us justice and equality." They have no aggressive designs toward other races or nations. The black nations of Africa and their black descendants who constitute the black minorities of the Americas are simply seeking what is their fair share of consideration for whatever men everywhere are entitled to. When the whites sometimes ask impatiently, "Well, what is it that they want?" they could easily understand it by asking themselves, "Just what is it that I want?" What the blacks want is EXACTLY THE SAME things the whites (and all people) want: no more, no less. Nothing else satisfies God's requirement. The blacks do not wish to "lord it over" anybody. Their persistent cry has ever been "Give us our fair share and we will shoulder our rightful responsibilities." All the black man has demanded is a chance to compete ON EQUAL TERMS. He disdains paternalism, tokenism, and most of all, welfare—a handout. Even when he is forced by an unjust system to accept these in order to survive, his sense of dignity is outraged and his heart bleeds. The balance in the hand of the rider of the black horse is no accident. And he did not usurp it. It was given to him by God. Backed by a Divine Providence, he has a mandate to establish justice and equality. Everywhere one turns today it is evident: in professional sports, in politics, in the United Nations. The present President of the United States of America owes his success in getting to be the Chief Executive to the black voters who hold the BALANCE of power at the polls. The Capitol City of the nation, Washington, has had only two Mayors since becoming self-governing. Both have been black.

In order to accomplish God's assignment to him, the rider of the black horse is told, to put "a measure (one) of wheat for a penny and three measures of barley for a penny" on the balances. This is a mandate because "a voice in the midst of the four beasts" said it. It must therefore "shortly come to pass" as all other things outlined in the Revelation. Why should there be one measure of wheat on one side of the balance and three measures of barley on the other? The emphasis was not on the number of measures but on the balance: Whatever it takes to bring the scale to a point of even balance, do it without regard for quantity on either side. This symbolizes that God's standard of justice is not quantitative as is man's, but is qualitative. Isaiah the prophet was sent to remind the people that Jehovah declares, "For my thoughts are not your thoughts, neither are your ways my ways, saith the Lord" (Isaiah 55:8). Man's standard of justice is invariably quantitative. He characteristically thinks that proportional representation is perfect justice. But when the cards have been stacked, the dice have been loaded to the advantage of one group, proportional representation adds one more weight to the disadvantaged. It is as if two men started out on a course: one with a weight tied to him and the other unencumbered. The one who is free travels faster and is soon far ahead of the other. Then, at a point, someone comes and says, "It is not fair for one man to be burdened down and the other free. I will remove the burden from the one held back by it. Then they will be equal." The flaw in this kind of thinking (and practice) is that it takes no account of the advantage of distance the unencumbered man has already. Unless the first man is retarded and/or the second one accelerated the two will never travel abreast of each other. Although they appear to be equal by virtue of their both now being unencumbered, the second man will always be "bringing up the rear" and always arriving late, after the distribution of goods has been completed or is well under way. He will be consigned to take the leavings. The positions of importance or advantage will have been filled by the time the late man qualifies. To bring about equality the man who has been held back needs three measures to the one of the man who has not been held back. The economically deprived need MORE than the ones who have had the advantages, at least until the scale is balanced. The children who have had to accept inferior education need better, not average, tutoring and facilities in order to overcome their disadvantage in the competition. The patient who has lost the most blood because of his wounds needs more blood than that other patient who had lost little or no blood. The wounds of the blacks have been many and deep in the competition in the international arena as well as on a personal individual basis. It is not enough to remove the restrictions: what is needed is a helping hand UNTIL THE SCALE IS BALANCED.

One more thing is different about the situation of the black horse as compared with the white and the red before him. It is that a warning was in his (the rider's) instructions: "And see thou hurt not the oil and the wine." Neither of the riders of the two previous horses heard a voice giving them precise instructions. The greater the responsibility, the greater the necessity for clear direction. The responsibility of the rider of the black horse is greater because of the very nature of the assignment: IT WAS SPIRITUAL. Anyone can conquer with physical weapons. Anyone can disturb the peace and destroy. But a peculiar discipline is required of those whose tasks are fundamentally spiritual.

"See thou hurt not the oil and the wine." What does this mean? I have heard various Bible teachers, preachers, and even theologians stumble over this passage in the Revelation without the slightest inkling of what it signifies. I, too, was for many years puzzled by it. But when the Holy Spirit took me through the book of Revelation and cleared my sight, it was crystal clear. You see, the rider of the black horse was given a spiritual mission (really commission) and was assured of God's support. But God does not support anybody or anything unconditionally. This is a pitfall of presumption into which many divinely-gifted men and women have fallen. To exercise divine authority or power one must walk a tightrope of personal discipline and strict obedience. "Not my will but Thine be done" is the very essence of sonship to God, the more so for those charged with heavy responsibilities. In the process of representing a Holy God who in His very Being is judgment (justice), truth and right (eousness), one must be spotless himself. "Who shall ascend into the hill of the Lord? or who shall stand in his holy place? He that hath clean hands and a pure heart. . ." (Ps. 24:3-4). "How wilt thou say to thy brother, Let me pull out the mote out of thine eye; first cast out the beam out of thine own eye; and then shalt thou see clearly to cast out the mote out of thy brother's eye" (Mat. 7:4, 5).

The oil and the wine referred to are spiritual symbols. They have nothing to do (as employed in this context) with famine or any other economic conditions. They symbolize the Divine Spirit through Whom the Power must come in order to get God's work done. "Except the Lord build the house, they labor in vain that build it" (Ps. 127:1). In the Old Testament, the pure oil of the olive was prescribed by God to symbolize His Spirit in the most important spiritual functions. It was prescribed (anointing with it) in the investiture of the priests into that sacred office; for they stood and mediated between God and man (Ps. 133:2). It was used to anoint the prophets who were called of God to be His spokesman to the people: "Thus saith the Lord." It was prescribed to fuel the perpetual light in the house of Jehovah as a symbol of His presence among His people. It was used to anoint kings at their accession to the throne.

The wine in Revelation 6:6 is likewise a spiritual symbol. It was used at the Passover supper. When Jesus gave a new meaning to the Passover supper, the commemoration of liberation from the slavery of sin, He applied it to the establishment of the new covenant in His blood. He, himself, being the sacrificial lamb without spot, went to the cross. Since His own blood was to be shed, Jesus told His disciples, "This (wine) is my blood of the new covenant" (St. Mark 14:24). Thus, the wine of the Passover festival was invested with a new (spiritual) meaning: Henceforth it would symbolize the very life essence of Jesus, the Savior from sin.

The admonition to "hurt not the oil and the wine" was given to the rider of the black horse to say "Don't disregard or turn your back on or leave God out of the picture in your pursuit of justice and equality." The battle, after all, is the Lord's. The great temptation is to regard the struggle for justice from a purely human or social viewpoint. We sometimes speak of "social justice" as a matter of ethics, with no relation to the Divine Order. It is social only inasmuch as it involves people. In a true sense, however, justice is spiritual. "The judgments of the Lord are true and righteous altogether" (Ps. 19:9). No amount of marching, protesting, picketing, boycotting, soliciting of endorsements by celebrities in the struggle, accepting donations for "the cause" from "the people with the big money," can be substituted for God's direct backing — the oil and the wine. The cause of justice and equality should be put forward by people who know God and whose lives are a testimony to His truth and righteousness. Otherwise the whole procedure becomes a mockery and doomed to ultimate futility. I have seen people of diverse affiliations marching in parades for justice and equality and shouting themselves hoarse with demands for them, but who, sadly, would not know Jesus Christ if He came and sat in their laps. I have seen people who are atheists, not believing that there is a God, pleading for justice to be done on behalf of the poor and disadvantaged, while it is only God's mercy that keeps them (the atheists) afloat. They have hurt the oil and the wine, shamefully polluting them. And those who claim to be godly, who join with those imposters, are "unequally yoked together," no matter how skillfully they may rationalize their behavior.

The rider of the black horse has a divine mandate to:

1 – Hold high the balance. Let his actions speak and let his voice be heard – everywhere there is injustice and/or inequality.

2 – Balance the scale, whatever it takes to do so (short of violence, of course). He must keep his hands off the balance when weighing the contents. He must not tip the scales on either side – must not compromise.

3 – Heed the warning: "Hurt not the oil and the wine," by sticking to strictly spiritual foundations and by rigid personal discipline. In the opening of the book of Revelation there was a church cited for censure "because thou has left thy first love" (Rev. 2:4). He must reject the lure of materialism, the white man's besetting fault. Some blacks have left the church for a lucrative entertainment career. This is a false god. He must, like Daniel the prophet and his companions, "refuse the king's dainties." He must escape the trap of racial integration based on social considerations. Both heaven and

hell are integrated; so integration in itself means nothing. He must reject out of hand the folly of black nationalism and black militantism. (Martin Luther King was a voice in the wilderness of violence.) He must be able to see through and avoid the subterfuge of neo-ecumenism that cloaks all who scream "Jesus" and base their authenticity on subjective experience at the expense of the complete word of God, while welcoming every diverse element under the umbrella.

The pale horse is the fourth and last in the series. Unlike all the others which preceded him, he has no definite color. There is a significant reason for this. He cannot be precisely identified because he is a "duke's mixture." He is so mixed up with so many different things that he can only be described as "a pale horse." I know the type so well. As a boy I lived through the last phase of the horse and buggy days. The people of that day had two terms for the pale horse: "motley" and "grizzly." This type was the result of interbreeding. They had no distinguishing characteristics except the mixture. These typified the "mongrel mutt," the "neither fish nor fowl," the "anything goes" syndrome.

In the sixth chapter of Revelation the pale horse represents integration – a fusion of diverse elements into one hodgepodge. There is a satanically induced trend toward the erasure of the lines of distinction between races, cultures, sexes, the sacred and the secular, and many other. The reason for this is that Satan is attempting to confuse the minds of people so as to make it easy for him to seduce them. There are so many commercial conglomerates today that one seldom knows whose product he is purchasing or using. Tuning in on the radio, one has to wait a while to know if he is listening to gospel music, blue grass, country western or disco. The standard hymns of the Christian faith are almost all in mothballs. Standing on the street in "anytown," one has to look closely and considerably long to know whether what he sees coming or going is male or female, the modes of dress and personal grooming are so similar. Imagine the confusion in the minds of children who cannot make the refinements necessary to worship or clown by the sounds coming from the radio or television. With the openness with which people are plugging for "gay rights," "women's lib," legalized marijuana, etc., it becomes increasingly difficult to raise a youngster with any sense of certainty about anything. The ecumenical movement, both classical and neo, threatens to wipe out doctrinal standards. They are making it harder and harder to continue in "the Apostles" doctrine and fellowship, and they seem to be oblivious to a "faith once delivered to the saints."

Strangely enough, the only rider who was given a name was the rider of the pale horse which had no definite mark of distinction. His name is death. It is most appropriate, for the horse on which he rides symbolizes confusion (literally con + fusion: with + joining together). Whenever diverse elements are heedlessly thrown together the result is confusion and at the end of the trail is death. Paleness is typical of sickness and death. Satan is the Apostle of Death, "a murderer from the beginning." "The wages of sin is death." So, as the rider (death) of the pale horse rode forth "hell followed with him." "God is not the author of confusion, but of peace..." (I Cor. 14:33). In this closing age of human history man is on a collision course. As standards—all standards—tend to melt away in a universal pot, you may be quite sure that death is the driver of the vehicle transporting on the joy ride and hell is the final destination. We are in the death throes of civilization "as sure as shootin'." "The coming of the Lord draweth nigh." And his kingdom must come with Him. The antichrist will probably make his appearance during the time of this pale horse which is shortly to dawn upon us. We are now living in the day of the black horse's ascendency.

Now for a summary of the four horses: What does it all signify? What overall meaning does it have when seen in proper perspective?

First, we are approaching the end of the age. This succession of horses indicates the ways and means by which the various changes will take place.

Second, each stage of the process will be characterized by more drastic and dramatic changes. The time frame for each phase is shortened. Before adjustments can be made to one it will be succeeded by the next demanding drastic readaptation.

Third, at the end of the fourth horse's ride Jesus Christ will return to earth and set up His kingdom, inaugurating the millennium: one thousand years of world peace.

Chapter Five

SOMETHING IN THE MELTING POT THAT WON'T MELT

As much as we hear and repeat the cliche in America: "The Melting Pot," it seldom dawns on anyone who employs the phrase that there is something in the melting pot that WILL NOT MELT. What is it? And why will it not melt? These are the questions which I am going to answer in this chapter.

The "something" that will not melt is the Negro, or black man. Everything nationality and racial wise that has made its home in the Americas has melted in the racial and nationality mix EXCEPT THE BLACKS. This is not to say that there are no racial or nationality minorities in America other than the blacks. The difference is that the members of other minorities have an option, a choice about their mixing and melting. The orientals, the hispanics, segregate by choice whenever it occurs. But they have upward mobility as a group in a manner and a degree denied the blacks. Millions of blacks in America who have been born there and who know no other place on earth they can call home are consistently denied privileges (indeed rights) other peoples from all over the world are freely accorded. Yes, I am fully aware of the Constitutional "guarantees" and the civil rights legislation of the last couple of decades. I am also painfully aware that legislation is one thing and implementation is quite another. No other legislation is so slowly, so deviously, so laboriously and so reluctantly implemented as that pertaining to the rights of the blacks. Take just one instance. The Supreme (highest and final) Court of the United States mandated that racial segregation in the public schools of the nation be eliminated "with all deliberate speed." Here it is nearly three decades later with the fact of racial segregation still all over the nation. If I were on death row, and the Supreme Court ORDERED my release "with all deliberate speed," and it still had not been complied with twenty-six years later, I think I would not be on death row but either dead or in an insane asylum. If I were alive at all and observed and heard those who were responsible for my release continually wrangling for such a period over HOW I should be released, I would be totally incompetent to function normally.

The blacks in the United States are still substantially apart from the mainstream of the American culture. "Oh, yes," I hear you object, "the blacks are Americans like everybody else." The first part of that statement is unquestionably true. The blacks are citizens of the U.S.A. But the last part of the statement — like everybody else — is undeniably false. The blacks can vote (at long last), they can own property (when it is cheap enough), they can hold public office (when the constituency represented is, with few exceptions, predominately black), they can own and operate businesses (on the small scale on the farthest fringes of the giant economic system). Do these conditions mean that the American blacks have effectively entered into the mainstream of the life of the nation? My answer is an emphatic NO.

Let us take housing. We now have open housing laws, even in the deep South. However, it is open AT BOTH

ENDS. So that as the blacks move in the whites move out. Since the integration of the public schools in the South (where the overwhelming majority of the blacks still live) I have watched "integrated" schools (with benefit of busing), revert to type and become white or black. This is the typical, not the exceptional, pattern. Even in the most advanced and "liberal" metropolitan centers of the East, the Midwest, and West you see organized protest and even bloody rioting when the blacks are brought into formerly white communities. They are being educated, alright, in the racism that keeps that certain something in the melting pot from melting: Boston, Los Angeles, Chicago, Pontiac, to name a few.

In employment, the blacks still constitute a wildly disproportionate percentage of the unemployed AT ANY TIME, and by the most sloppily-kept statistics. Why is this true in a country where there are ON THE BOOKS the finest non-discriminatory laws in the civilized world? They are ON THE BOOKS. And they stay there. It might be likened to the situation of the man whose friend asked "Why do you live alone?" The reply was "But I don't live alone." The man pointed to a beautiful portrait on the wall. It was, he said, his companion. "See," said he, "she is always here when I come home. She is always smiling no matter what's wrong in my world. I have her here for dinner every day." "Yes," replied the questioner, "but you have no real LIVE relationship. She cannot hold your hand or speak. She cannot bear you children. And she has the same smile for everybody who comes around. In other words, she's not really yours in a true sense." Every high public executive pledges to "do something about the unemployment situation." Well, they usually do, where the blacks are concerned: They either study it to death or accentuate or aggravate the condition. Effective melting means unrestricted job opportunity. There is something in the melting pot that won't melt.

Let's not even seriously mention intermarriage of the races. Here, again, there is an unwritten law, a "gentlemen's agreement," among the whites OF ALL NATIONALITY BACKGROUNDS. I have seen it from many vantage points of observation. It is the norm. Blacks and whites who work side by side, who have common educational, cultural, and other interests, who enjoy one another's company genuinely, close a door at checkout time. The friendships that develop on the job and provide a continuing fellowship off the job so normally and naturally among whites (and among blacks) are aborted and "contained" between blacks and whites who work in the same places doing the same jobs. I have "white friends" with whom I am completely congenial who have never accepted an invitation nor followed an impulse to "drop by sometime." Nor have they had me to join them in a social function unless it was "something special." Mind you, these "friends" would be disconcerted, perhaps truly hurt, if I were to call this to their attention. So we go on enjoying a nice friendship WITHIN THE ZONES OF AGREEMENT in our society. The "special" occasions are not normal. It's similar to visiting a zoo. Enjoy the animals occasionally. Even feed and talk kindly to and smile at them. But KEEP THEM CONTAINED AT A SAFE DISTANCE. Otherwise they might cause harm to you. I have watched the parents of small children of whites and of blacks when they meet by chance in a typical situation—the street, the supermarket, the bus, etc. How relaxed the parents of both are, usually falling into conversation quite easily and unselfconsciously. Then I have observed the small children of blacks and whites meeting under the same circumstances. The children are as unselfconscious as their parents had been. But almost invariably the white parents will tense up and exhibit anxiety, even when they try to disguise it with artificial smiles and hollow-sounding words of tolerance to the perfectly uninhibited youngsters. I have noted the (sometimes audible) sigh of relief when the episode ended. I know there are beautiful exceptions, but I emphasize the rule is as I have stated.

In the world of religious affairs, it is the same, or even more pronounced. There is something in the melting pot that will not melt. "The most racially-segregated hour in America is Sunday morning from eleven to twelve o'clock." Check it out. It amuses (sometimes disgusts) me to hear so many whites pleading for conservation of (gasoline) energy while pointing out the great waste from public school busing. They are great proponents of "the neighborhood school" arrangement. Yet these same whites advocate busing children just as far to white church-sponsored schools all week. And they seem to like that type of busing so well that they still bus adults and children long distances on Sundays (past many neighborhood churches of their own denomination), with never a thought of "wasting gas," while the public school busing has stopped at least for the weekend.

There is a growing trend among American white church congregations to accept blacks into membership of formerly all-white churches. Negroes are justly and understandably suspicious of such overtures. Still a comparatively few blacks do "join." It turns out, however, that what they are joining is not the church, but a sort of religious club where you pay your dues and make the meetings. What's really happening is that the blacks are being "taken in" but not into the fellowship of the Christian family. The story is told of two white pastors who knew each other casually and met at a denominational convention where the subject of receiving blacks into membership was in prominence on the agenda. Between sessions, one asked the other, "Henry, how many blacks has your church 'taken in'?" The other, knowing the prejudice of his friend, replied, "We haven't 'taken in' any blacks but I suppose we must have about a third of the congregation black members. We don't keep statistics on this and I've never made a count personally."

Blacks who join "white" church congregations are still in a controlled situation in a white society. Only they are now enjoying a subtle, more sophisticated form of racism and discrimination. But it's not painful because they have been given the anesthetic that desensitizes them to the operation. It is a sad fact that virtually the only times they will enjoy real fellowship is at the worship services and at a few special functions that take place at the church plant. When these are over, the blacks go back to their black world and the whites go back to theirs. Strangely, the white members have a carryover fellowship in their homes and (usually white) neighborhoods. There is a conspicuous absence of that very potent spiritual state of affairs which marks the truly Apostolic church: "And all that believed were together, and had all things common.... And they, continuing daily with one accord in the temple, AND BREAKING BREAD FROM HOUSE TO HOUSE, did eat their food with gladness and singleness of heart" (Acts 2:44-46). There is a tacit assumption in such churches that, at least within the lifetime of most of the present members, there will be no black pastor or other high church officers except on a de facto quota or token principle.

It amuses (sometimes disgusts) me as I watch the white "electronic church" on television. Blacks (poor as most of them are) are helping to promote the programs to the tune of millions of dollars. Yet they must watch a "show" where the participation of blacks is either excluded or rigidly controlled. There is something in the melting pot that won't melt. Recently, while my wife and I were on vacation, we went out of our way to visit a multimillion dollar community developed and paid for by mostly the voluntary contributions of television viewers of one of America's most renowned and comprehensive religious networks. Needless to say, a substantial amount of the money that built that community was supplied by blacks. Yet the only black person we saw during our stay there was pumping gas. Almost any secular community of comparable size would have had a much higher percentage.

These are the facts, like it or not. But why? What are the real, not the imaginary, causes of this very real separation in American life as far as blacks and whites are concerned? Number one: purely and simply, The United States of America is primarily, fundamentally, indubitably, undeniably irrefutably, incontrovertably, and INEXCUSABLY, a racist nation. This harks back to the influence of the Anglo-Saxon. This disease (ingrained ideas of racial superiority and supremacy) seems to be native to the Anglo-Saxon blood. It seems ineradicable from the British psyche. Long before the Nazis under Adolph Hitler pursued the notion to ridiculous and embarrassing extremes, the white horse which "went forth conquering and to conquer" (Rev. 6:2), the British had foisted upon the world the insidious virus of race prejudice. I am not asserting that they invented it. Race prejudice has been in existence from very ancient times. It is a part of the Bible record: "And Joseph made haste.... And he washed his face, and went out, and refrained himself, and said, Set on bread. And they set on for him by himself, and for them by themselves, and for the Egyptians, which did not eat with him, by themselves: because the Egyptians might not eat bread with the Hebrews: for that is an abomination to the Egyptians" (Genesis 43:30-32).

Since Genesis is the very first book of the Bible, and since the event referred to here took place before Israel became a nation, we may safely conclude it was very ancient times. No, I emphatically repeat it: the Anglo-Saxons did not INVENT race prejudice. What I maintain just as emphatically, is that the facts of history support it that they peddled it around the world and made studied and persistent effort to perpetuate it throughout civilization. Like a prostitute with a loathesome physical disease who infects all who traffic with her, and can actually start an epidemic, the Anglo-Saxon exported a philosophy (and practical way of life) of racial superiority to the far-flung extent of the greatest (and last) of the world's great empires. It reached epidemic proportions everywhere the British flag was planted. It threatened the destruction of civilization in Nazi Germany, the worst "case-history" instance of the disease on record. It dies hardest in those places in the world where the English language and cultural heritage prevail. It has seeped into "every crack and cranny" wherever the Anglo-Saxon INFLUENCE is felt, the religious establishment being no exception. The white man (as a whole) will, when the necessity of survival demands it, tolerate and learn to live with almost any arrangement in human affairs so long as he can figure out a way to exercise THE CONTROLLING INTEREST. He simply cannot tolerate or accommodate the idea (and practice) that he can function in a situation where the leadership and control are in non-white hands. This spiritual disease is the great crippler responsible for all of the major problems of western civilization today. And upon its cure rests the peace and tranquility of the international community.

Here I am a pessimist. The disease will not be cured. A certain amount of containment, yes, but not a cure. That will come when the Millennium Kingdom of God is ushered in at Jesus Christ's coming again. And the time draws near.

I am writing this book to bring out the point that in spite of the fact that the collapse of civilization, the destruction of the world, is going to be the ultimate harvest from the "Anglo-Saxon's Syndrome," God has not left Himself without witnesses during the buildup. The black horse will not "save the day" or "right the wrongs" that have been perpetrated by the white (or, by catalytic action, the red) horse. The function which God has mandated to the black horse is to emblazon it upon the record that "the judgments (justice) of the Lord (Jehovah) are true and righteous altogether" (Ps. 19:9). Jesus once denounced the Scribes and Pharisees of His day because they emphasized tithing and omitted the "weightier matters of the law, judgment (justice), mercy, and faith" (Mat. 23:23). The black man's WITNESS in this regard, by word and example will help to "prepare the way of the Lord" at His second coming. When the way was prepared for the Lord's first coming, it was accomplished not by the recognized, sophisticated, well-trained leadership from the precincts of the highly-organized institutionalized religion of that day. Rather it was from a crude, rough-cut, definitely strong-voiced John the Baptist who was a "voice in the wilderness." He not only stripped himself of food, clothing and shelter, to bare essentials, but he reduced the religion of Israel to its essence: "to do justly, to love mercy, and to walk humbly. . . ." The blacks of this generation must, in the Spirit of Jesus Christ, rescue the Christian faith from the pious professions of priest-craft and the "program" mania of the laity. They must in simplicity and utter sincerity demonstrate the reality of God in the ordinary life situations of the multitudes who are on the lowest level of society. Rejecting the "celebrity complex" and the "prosperity formula," they must show the world what Divine Love is. Their white brothers in the faith have all but forfeited their right to do so. They have been too preoccupied with compromises with the present world (ly) system to detect that their religious institutions have taken on the salient characteristics of their secular counterparts. God has uniquely situated the blacks of the world, who have the least vested interest in the spiritually bankrupt status quo, to set the prime example. They must remember that Jesus came "to preach the gospel to the POOR," not because they are poor, but because Divine Love is the real solution to poverty. Human (selfish) love is its cause.

Secondly, the blacks were brought to the New World under force and duress, not of their own volition. The psychological impact of that fact alone is tremendous. Consider some of the ramifications. The enslavement of the African in the New World involved the farthest mass population transplant in history. Sheer distance made all possibility of getting back home impossible. A determined, calculated effort at mass deculturation was carried out. There was an effort to erase the culture of the native land and enforce adaptation to that of the dominant (white) group; at least in rudimentary form. The effort was unsuccessful, however. Like Israel, there has been a reversion to type. We alluded to this earlier.

Unlike other minorities in America, the Afro-American has no specific nationality base with which he can identify. The Jew has Israel, the Mexican-American has Mexico, the Indian is at home in the land of his fathers in quite familiar territory, the Japanese-American has Japan, the Chinese-American has China; even the most recent arrivals on the scene, the Indo-Chinese, have their countries of origin to which they can point. But the Afro-American has a vague notion of where on the vast continent of Africa his roots are and what his present-day relatives are doing. Being legally citizens in America, but being denied full acceptance, he is afloat – the land-based "boat-people" in a vast sea where the navigation and the location of the specific perils are far more difficult. Even the chances of "rescue" are more limited as their plight is less vivid. For the Afro-American there is no place to turn for refuge or redress except to America which still rejects his claim to all the blessings of liberty.

Contrast this situation with that of the whites. The families of the white immigrants who came to America came with a known welcome and the POSITIVE MIND SET of expecting to better their lot. They were therefore psychologically prepared to endure the rigorous competition in a free society while en route to their place on the totem pole. Everywhere they went they felt encouraged to fight on. "You can make it" is what they felt at every hardship, for they had role models who had come up from their own ranks and who had preceded them in overcoming the normal difficulties with which they were still beset. Contrast this with the situation of the blacks. They were snatched away with no positive preparation; their families were deliberately broken up at the auction block so that they could not encourage one another, pull together and boost one another's morale. With all the hard adjustments they were obliged to make just to survive as individuals, new family relationships were forced upon them, often for the undisguised purpose of breeding good stock for the work of the plantation. Then they were deprived of an opportunity for an education (it was a criminal offense in some states to teach a slave to read and write). Yet education is an essential tool for effective citizenship in a free society.

Thirdly, after the emancipation (a better term would be new slavery) of the blacks was accomplished by legal decree, almost the entire white American society rejected the blacks as full citizens. Their labor, almost all menial and unskilled, was wanted, but little or nothing else was. The white man's dilemma was "How can we take advantage of this vast reservoir of cheap labor without allowing the blacks to interfere with the other things that are meaningful to us?" The solution that was finally universally accepted was segregation: "Keep him (the blacks) to himself except when he is making a contribution to our security, and even then keep him under strict scrutiny." The ghetto was written into the law in the southern states. In the rest of the nation it became the unwritten law, no less effective. The principle and practice of racial segregation kept something in the melting pot which it at the same time kept from melting.

In the fourth place, the extremely high visibility of the Negro — his immediate easy identification — set him up for a target of deprivation and abuse. The whites, of whatever diverse background (and to a lesser extent other minorities), had one thing in common that gave them acceptance and therefore an opportunity to advance in accordance with their individual abilities. That common thing was a fair complexion. The only place a Negro could "hide" was in a black situation. Italian, Swede, Englishman, Irishman, Hungarian, Pole, Spaniard, Portuguese, German, Frenchman, Russian, Syrian, Jew, South American, Canadian, etc., had not this badge of approbium: the black skin. Still there have come into America blacks from all of the above-named nationality groups, only to be evaluated and treated with a diabolical uniformity in the struggle for existence. There is something in the melting pot that won't melt.

You may say, "But stick to your subject. After all, you

are talking about Africa." I hasten to assure you I'm sticking quite closely to the subject. For Africa has come to have a symbolic as well as a literal meaning. All that I have said with reference to the black American descendants of Africans is applicable to Africa in the larger context of the community of nations. Until comparatively recently, African nations and colonial subjects were hardly taken seriously in any international conclave. Yet the resources of Africa constituted so much of the world's industrial lifeblood that they were practically indispensable. There is a common thread that connects Africa and her three offspring in the New World: the three large black population centers of Brazil, the Caribbean, and the United States of America. They have remained African in essential culture and have this one thing in common, viz., their intactness. They have remained a lump. In the Caribbean Islands, until recently, a mere handful of whites from overlord governments have kept the races separate. As Brazil, for politically and economically expedient reasons, aligns herself more and more with the powerful nations of the Americo-European group, it becomes more and more difficult for the black segment of the population to find their way out of a de facto caste complex.

This brings me to a point where it is expedient to bring out a biblical reference to this matter. There is a parallel between the sixth chapter of Revelation and the seventh chapter of Daniel at important points. In Revelation there are four horses. We have already indicated what they represent. In Daniel, instead of four horses the symbolism takes the form of four different animals. They have the same significance as the four horses. Let us see: "Daniel spake and said, I saw in my vision by night, and, behold, the four winds of heaven strove upon the great sea. And four great beasts came up from the sea, diverse one from another. The first was like a lion, and had eagle's wings: I beheld until the wings thereof were plucked, and it was lifted from the earth, and made stand upon the feet as a man. And a man's heart was given to it. And behold another beast, a second, like a bear, and it raised up itself on one side, and it had three ribs in the mouth of it between the teeth of it: and they said thus unto it, Arise, devour much flesh. After this I beheld, and lo another, like a leopard, which had upon the back of it four wings of a fowl; the beast had also four heads; and dominion was given to it. After this I saw in the night visions, and behold a fourth beast, dreadful and terrible, and strong exceedingly; and it had great iron teeth: it devoured and brake in pieces, and stamped the residue with the feet of it: and it was diverse from all the beasts that were before it; and it had ten horns" (Daniel 7:2-7).

In Revelation the first horse was white; in Daniel the first beast was like a lion. They both refer to the white (Caucasian) race and western civilization (which was developed by the white race). In Daniel the description is more explicit. There the beast has eagle's wings, they were plucked (off), the beast stood upright as a man although it was a lion, and a man's heart was given to it. What does all this mean? Great Britain gave us our last great empire and it was the most farflung of them all — even Rome. It, the British Empire, was conceived, engineered, and maintained by the white race. That is the significance of the eagle's wings on the lion: the British Empire was far-flung. The eagle is known for distance flying and endurance in flight. The bow and arrows of the rider of the white horse in Revelation symbolizes the same thing. Britain's seal of state is a lion (standing upright on its hind legs). The two wings are the two English-speaking, British-cultured nations that span almost the entire North American continent: Canada and the United States. These wings flew England, the Mother country, across the vast Atlantic Ocean where English culture took root. However, the wings were plucked off – severed. Canada and the United States became independent of the imperial government. A man's heart was given to this beast. This signifies that although the beast, to put it as did Revelation, "went forth conquering and to conquer," (conquest was the PRIMARY aim), still it was a benign and benevolent blessing: the white man, primarily under English initiative and sponsorship, has brought great blessings to humanity: a beast with a HUMAN heart. A beast in terms of the great military thrusts and political subjugation of other peoples, yet a humane benefactor in terms of extending the blessings of liberty through institutions oriented to human rights and service. Western civilization is the last and the greatest. Daniel's prophecy that in the last days "many shall run to and fro, and knowledge shall be increased (flourish)" (Daniel 12:4) is fulfilled in the unfolding of western civilization, which is white. This is the civilization which gave to the world mechanization, aerodynamics, mass production, industrial management, electronics, hydrolics, thermodynamics, business conglomerates, and so many chemical marvels. Space exploration and the atomic researches climax the whole process. Like a brilliant meteor, however, it is burning itself out as it races across an illuminated sky.

The second beast was like a bear. What could be plainer: in Revelation the second horse was red. The Communists are universally dubbed reds. Russia, the developer and extender of Communism, is symbolized as a bear in present-day parlance. We speak of "the Russian bear." The bear had three ribs in his teeth in Daniel's account. These are the three nations in the prophecy of Ezekiel (38:5) which Russia infiltrates and takes over just prior to the Russian invasion of Israel (Palestine). They are Libya, Ethiopia, and Persia (Iran).

The third beast in Daniel was like a leopard. This one parallels the black horse of Revelation. It is the black African leopard that is referred to, not the spotted variety. This is the black panther which was the symbol adopted by the American black militant organization of the same name (Black Panthers) of the nineteen sixties. Those who founded and guided the Black Panthers probably did not know why they adopted this symbol, but like the red label on the Communists, it was in the Providence of God and the prophecy of the Bible. Although the Black Panthers were militant and advocated violence, they were motivated by a burning desire for justice and equality (the balance). They, unfortunately, failed to heed the warning, "Hurt not the oil and the wine." As a consequence, they failed miserably.

The fourth beast in Daniel's prophecy, just as the fourth horse in Revelation, was without a definite name (in Revelation with no specific color). It was not lion, or bear, or leopard, just a beast. Here again, paralleling Revelation's pale horse we have the nondescript "mongrel mutt," "neither fish nor fowl," "anything goes," "hodgepodge-Dukes-mixture" type. As in Revelation, so in Daniel this last beast is a juggernaut of wasting and destruction: "dreadful," "terrible," "strong exceedingly," "great iron teeth." It "devoured," "brake in pieces," "stamped the residue with the feet. . . ." The fourth beast had ten horns. These, of course, are the ten European nations that are grounded in the old Roman Empire and which will try to revive its power in the world, not primarily by military means, but by politico-economic. Their big power base is the Common Market. Personally, I believe that the antichrist will emerge from this confederation, for, as in Revelation, this fourth beast sets up the world stage for the return of Jesus Christ. Another feature of this fourth beast in Daniel's prophecy is that "it had great iron teeth." This is not to be confused with the iron LEGS of the image in the dream of Nebuchadnezzar, which symbolizes the Roman Empire (Dan. 2:33). The LEGS are the MARCHING Roman legions that went in conquest throughout the then-known world and subdued. The iron TEETH are symbolic of the complete destructive power of this fourth beast. The function of TEETH is to GRIND UP, to CRUSH, to MASTICATE. Substances thoroughly chewed, form an amalgam in which none of the components are clearly distinguishable. This parallels precisely the symbolic significance of the pale horse in Revelation. There, "hell followed. . . ," in Daniel, the maw engulfed (hell enlarged her mouth). This is that fusion process already alluded to. Iron teeth insures their efficiency to do the job. Nothing will be excepted in the grinding process—no element in the culture. Thus, while the iron teeth do belong (in the larger context) to Rome, the emphasis here is upon the great destruction at the last stages rather than (as in the case of the legs) upon identifying the world power.

Of peculiar interest in conjunction with this subject of Africa's role is Daniel's observation that the (black) leopard had four wings and four heads. Africa and her three sons (black population centers) across the seas are the objects of reference.

In the present state of affairs, worldwide, and in America, Africa has "come to the kingdom for just such a time as this." The stage is perfectly prepared. Africa is by the Providence of God cast in the role of being the conscience of the civilized world. The besetting fault of the white race, who more than any other built this magnificent civilization, is egotism. Enthralled at the great successes in building it, he has forgotten his plain human frailties. Like the fabled Narcissus, he has become enarmored with his own splendor and has settled down to gazing in self-admiration in a mirror. He has become victim of the illusion which sooner or later traps all wielders of great power over men. He ASSUMES superiority appropos of nothing more than his identification with the works of his hands which have wrought so well. One of the sons of England, a statesman at the zenith of her imperial glory, uttered a prophetic piece. I refer to the "Recessional" of Rudyard Kipling:

> God of our fathers, known of old,
>   Lord of our far-flung battle-line,
> Beneath whose awful Hand we hold
>   Dominion over palm and pine —
> Lord God of Hosts, be with us yet,
>   Lest we forget — lest we forget!
>
> The tulmult and the shouting dies;
>   The Captains and the kings depart:
> Still stands Thine ancient sacrifice,
>   An humble and a contrite heart.
> Lord God of Hosts, be with us yet,
>   Lest we forget —lest we forget!
>
> Far-called, our navies melt away;
>   On dune and headland sinks the fire:
> Lo, all our pomp of yesterday
>   Is one with Nineveh and Tyre!
> Judge of the Nations, spare us yet,
>   Lest we forget —lest we forget!

> If, drunk with sight of power, we loose
> Wild tongues that have not Thee in awe,
> Such boastings as the Gentiles use,
> Or lesser breeds without the Law —
> Lord God of Hosts, be with us yet,
> Lest we forget — lest we forget!
>
> For heathen heart that puts her trust
> In reeking tube and iron shard,
> All valiant dust that builds on dust,
> And, guarding, calls not Thee to guard,
> For frantic boast and foolish word —
> Thy mercy on Thy People, Lord!

Adolph Hitler and the Nazi philosophy of history and government gave visible expression to this fallacious weakness. Just as a great fault, geologically speaking, causes an eventual earthquake, just so this fault, racially speaking, caused the holocaust that wreaked havoc on the European continent where the philosophy was spawned, and its tremors reverberated around the world. Its ashes settled everywhere. The ridiculous extremes to which the Nazis pushed it, and the tragic results for the world, are but a logical consequence of that disease that ultimately infects the psyche of all who work or fight their way to a position where at last no visible challenger looms on the horizon. Humility becomes an obsolescence to be swept away with other debris in the ongoing process of "bigger and better." Alexander is said to have wept when there were no more worlds to conquer. Nero is reported to have fiddled while Rome burned. It seemed oblivious to the former that he might have employed his genius to perfecting that world he had conquered, once it was at his feet, wholly in his grasp. It seemed equally an irrelevancy to the latter that he might still have salvaged the best in his empire had he seriously addressed himself to the task of trying to understand and direct the raw energies and aspirations of the broad population base which constituted the real strength of the empire.

The corrective for this fatal fault must come from the outsider, or the system will self-destruct. That is why there is something in the melting pot that won't melt. There is something in this western civilization that is worth saving, by the Grace of God. Western civilization is with all its flaws, Christian. In terms of its affirmations, its commitments, and the basic substance of its institutions, it is the wave of the future. Unlike all previous empires that have waxed and waned under the judgment of God, this civilization is destined to be the one to "prepare the way of the Lord."

The PURITANS were Christian idealists lured by the vision of a society in which Christ would be the central reality. This vision inspired the dedication, the discipline that have left their mark on everything that can in any sense be called American. The ship that brought the PILGRIMS to the shores of the New World, Salem, significantly, means "peace," and this was a focal point of early settlement upon the land. Philadelphia is the "city of brotherly love." The thirteen original states symbolize Christ and the twelve Apostles. So it was that the nation of the United States of America was launched.

There are inherent values in western civilization that God has implanted which qualifies it for cleansing and salvaging. Believe it or not, these values do not include capitalistic free-enterprise. God is not the God of patterns but of principles. This was the crux of the difficulty when Jesus confronted the guardians of the Law of Moses. The traditions had come to occupy a more important place than the welfare of those they were supposed to protect. Institutional forms had come to be "sacred cows," sleek and fat, roaming among the spiritually impoverished people who supported them. Thus Jesus sought to separate the grain from the chaff by asserting ". . . you . . . transgress the commandment of God by your tradition" (Mat. 15:3). Again: "No man putteth a piece of new cloth unto an old garment, for that which is put in to fill it up taketh from the garment, and the rent is made worse. Neither do men put new wine into old bottles: else the bottles break, and the wine runneth out, and the bottles perish; but they put new wine into new bottles, and both are preserved" (Mat. 9:16-17). Western civilization, although Christian, is on a collision course. It is THE CHRIST SPIRIT, not the economic or political STRUCTURE which is AT THE BASE and AT THE HEART of western culture. That is what renders it salvageable. For the accomplishment of the task God has sent forth (the rider of) the black horse. That is why, in God's own Providence, that something in the melting pot WAS NOT SUPPOSED TO MELT. It is the catalytic agent which must swing the reaction in the right direction.

"For just such a time as this" Africa has not on its record any large-scale wars of mass destruction. There are no Genghis Khans, Napoleons, Stalins or Hitlers, no world wars (one nor two). In two world wars we have seen the wholesale destruction of some of the greatest treasures of architecture and other art of western civilization. The very nations that produced these treasures are the ones who destroyed them. The very term "vandalism," which has been coined to denote wanton destruction, derives its name from one of the European tribes that helped to destroy the Roman Empire. The destruction of the great renowned library of Alexandria,

Egypt, is a monument to the folly of unbridled ambition for conquest. There has been no African holocausts that can begin to compare with those perpetrated by modern European nations—no long-range, calculated wholesale destruction. The white man's scientific genius has brought us to the brink of atomic obliteration of civilization. Nowhere in the annals of human history do we find, as we do in Africa, so immense a land with a history of so little destruction (of property and resources) for so long a period. This fact alone should credential the people of this centre of the earth for a place in the topmost councils of the nations where they may be listened to with the utmost respect on that most common need of all mankind: PEACE.

The blacks must address themselves to the task, taking the risks that inevitably ensue. It is the last best hope. At the risk of being judged by the whites as blasphemously audacious and laughed out of court, the black man must put forth the effort in the spirit of "if I perish, I perish."

Great discipline is required even in preparation for the undertaking. He must keep himself "unspotted from the world," i.e., from the white man's vices. In nonconformity to the fads, mass movements, and amoral values swirling around him, he must demonstrate a lifestyle that reflects "that good, and acceptable, and perfect will of God." He must be scrupulously careful not to be guilty of that sin of presumption which says, "Let me pull out the mote that is in thine eye; when behold, there is a beam in thine own eye" (Mat. 7:4). In preparation for his special role, the black man must divest himself of the last vestiges of hypocrisy. He must guard against the tendency to "follow the crowd." The false prophet has perfected the art of the legendary pied piper with "good words and fair speeches" (Rom. 16: 18). The religious (or any other type of) racketeer must be known by one criterion: his fruits. Is he Christlike? IN SPIRIT? The black man must guard against becoming a white man within, with only his face black. I have traveled the length and breadth of America. In recent years I have observed a curious phenomenon: white manufacturers are advertising and appealing to blacks for their patronage by taking white mannequins and merely painting them dark. All the Caucasian features are there, unchanged. Aside from this being a prima facie insult to self-respecting blacks, it subtly and sinisterly puts forth a philosophy that the acceptable black must really be white beneath the superficial layer of pigment. Why haven't the manufacturers produced some mannequins with typical black features? Why have not the black patrons demanded it?

To be the conscience of western Christian culture, indeed requires rigid spiritual discipline. It must begin with the blacks within their own group. They must challenge Christian Europe and America to live up to what God requires and non-Christians in general to live up to their commitments as set forth in such documents as Magna Carta, the Declaration of Independence and Constitution of the United States of America. The hangups of white Christians (and whites in general) must be continually exposed and denounced. This denunciation must not take the (worldly) form of blatant demonstration but that of very simply stating the truth anywhere and everywhere it is obviously being denied. The Achilles' heel of the white church is its hangup on racial equality. That false pride of race that refuses stubbornly to yield even in religious circles to the Spirit of Christ must be challenged without ceasing by the blacks who are brothers in Christ. That something in the "white mind" that dictates that whites must hold the controlling interest, the trump card, in every situation where he functions must be denounced for what it is—a trick of satan to insure a schism in the Body of Christ, thereby reducing its effectiveness. This is wrong. And the whites must be made to see it with unjaundiced eye. The blacks must be without prejudices and hangups themselves. Every so-called black church should be seriously disturbed as long as it remains black. The witnessing of black Christians must be directed to all and sundry. I recall one Sunday when a junior high school youngster asked of me at church, "Rev. King, why we don't have any white people in our church?" It was a good question, and I congratulated this girl for being both so discerning and concerned. Then I asked her, "Do you have white kids at your school?" She replied, "Yes sir; lots of them." I followed with another question, "Have you ever invited any of them to come to your church?" She answered, "No sir." Now this girl had been responsible for bringing several other friends to our church. Yet it never occurred to her to invite the white youngsters to come with her. So I urged her to do so. As I was driving the van which customarily transported the youngsters to and from church, en route home we were passing a small group of white youth. The girl in reference said, "Rev. King, there go some white people. Let's invite them to church." I said, "Good, why not?" and hit the brakes. Several of the youngsters and I got out, approached them and made our witness (the approach being made by the young people). I can truthfully say that at our worship services we have had both black and white present every Sunday for the last three and a half years. This is especially gratifying since ours is a very small congregation.

For the sake of BALANCING THE SCALE, black Christians must be willing to be misunderstood and to suffer abuse. All violence and retaliatory methods must be eliminated at the source. Being defamed, they must intreat; being wronged, they must suffer it: turn the other cheek, go the second mile. They must "DEMONSTRATE that they are the children of their Father who is in heaven..." (Mat. 5:45). This demonstration of spiritual discipline must not be confused with that expediency technique known as the "Uncle Tom" and the "Aunt Jemima." This is most important. Although their outward dress and behavior may appear the same to the superficial observer, there is a basic difference. The blacks who perform the service of conscience guardian for their white fellow-Christians are ministering to them. They must therefore "speak the truth IN LOVE" (Eph. 4:15), "Endeavoring to keep the unity of the Spirit in the bond of peace" (Eph. 4:3). The blacks must not flatter, cringe, or compromise the truth. They must not supinely acquiesce to any wrongdoing for any advantage, personal or collective, but must face the truth and present it without self-abasement. They must always point up and point out wrongs from a BIBLICAL PERSPECTIVE, not from a social, economic, political, or any other. They must do this fearlessly, even under threats by the wrongdoer. They must be willing to don "sackcloth and ashes."

Be under no illusion. The blacks who function in the role described will not save civilization as a whole. They will not bring about racial or world peace on a grand scale. Only the coming of Jesus Christ, the Prince of Peace, will effect this. The blacks who will walk in the footsteps of Jesus are called to be faithful witnesses. They will constitute in our generation (the terminal one) "a remnant according to the election of grace" (Rom. 11:5). These must, like Daniel refuse "the king's dainties." The blacks will not all carry out the mandate. There are those who will not see the necessity for any such approach as this, especially as regards the disciplinary aspect. There are other blacks who, seeing the need, will not believe that it will do any good. These will remain in the throes of the frustration already at work wreaking disintegration upon their black victims in terms of vice, crime and moral depravity in general. They will continue to suffer in spite of all efforts to the contrary. There are still other blacks who will not accept their God-appointed role because they will feel they have beat the game—they have arrived because they have received their slice of the pie. These will regard the true peacemakers among them as stupid, holding them in utter disdain and contempt. To them, the blacks who accept the role of suffering redemptive service will appear not only silly and naive, but as disgusting reminders of a past which the nouveau-sophisticates would like to erase from memory. Then there are still others who will not have the courage nor the will to submit to the discipline required.

In spite of all obstructions and disparagements, however, these dedicated ones will carry out the mandate of God in these last days. A REMNANT will prevail. Their witness is all important. Crime, drug abuse, abortion, homosexuality, alcoholism, gambling will continue to plague the larger society, but a large minority will escape these pollutions. These vices have never had large-scale practice in Africa, and they have taken hold among Afro-Americans only as they have been corrupted by Caucasians.

The blacks have a mission to the White House, not to paint it black (as some militants, secular and religious, would do), but to purify it: eliminate the grey spots caused by the dust and grime of halfheartedness, special privilege, imperial design, and aristocratic arrogance. "But who are YOU, THE BLACKS, OF ALL PEOPLE, to tell us what's wrong and to tell US what to do?" I hear some of the offended saying. Well, it was once said of One judged by the powers that be, "Physician, heal thyself." But, in time, "the stone which the builders rejected is become the chief cornerstone: this is the Lord's doing, and it is marvellous in our eyes" (Ps. 118: 22-23).

The ugly duckling became a beautiful swan. The unsightly hideous toad became a charming prince. The beautiful butterfly unfolded its wings in the sunlight and soared after a period as a worm squirming in dark confinement. The bottom rail eventually came to the top. The phoenix rose from its own ashes. Yes, all this takes place when, in the fullness of time— the ripeness of God's Providence—it is so determined. "Can there any good thing come out of Nazareth?" Well, THE BEST THING IN THE WORLD came out of Nazareth! Despised and rejected.

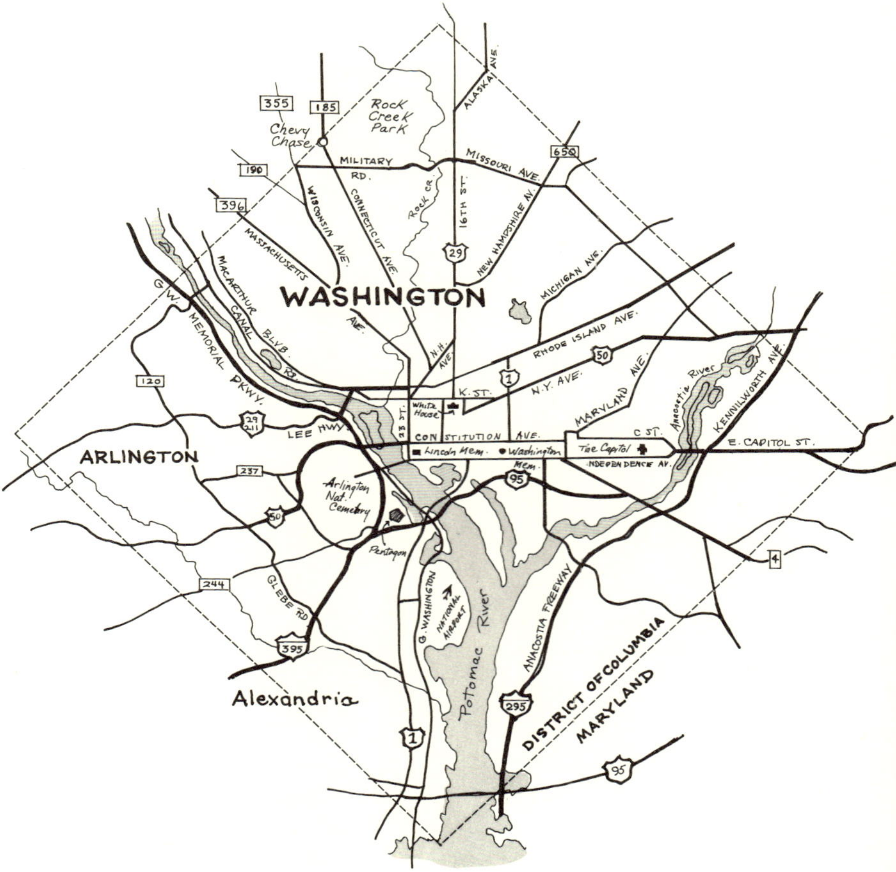

355
185
Rock Creek Park
Chevy Chase
MILITARY RD.
MISSOURI AVE.
ALASKA AVE.
650
190
396
WISCONSIN AVE.
CONNECTICUT AVE.
Rock Cr.
16TH ST.
NEW HAMPSHIRE AV.
29
MASSACHUSETTS AVE.
MACARTHUR BLVD.
CANAL RD.
G.W. MEMORIAL PKWY.
WASHINGTON
MICHIGAN AVE.
RHODE ISLAND AVE.
N.H. AVE.
50
1
K. ST.
N.Y. AVE.
MARYLAND AVE.
Anacostia River
KENILWORTH AVE.
120
29 211
LEE HWY.
23 ST.
White House
CONSTITUTION AVE.
C ST.
E. CAPITOL ST.
ARLINGTON
Lincoln Mem.
Washington Mem.
The Capitol
INDEPENDENCE AV.
237
Arlington Nat. Cemetery
95
50
Pentagon
4
244
GLEBE RD
G. WASHINGTON
NATIONAL AIRPORT
Potomac River
ANACOSTIA FREEWAY
395
Alexandria
295
DISTRICT OF COLUMBIA
MARYLAND
1
95

Chapter Six

THE NEW WORLD, AMERICA THE BEAUTIFUL, THE CITY FOURSQUARE

When the first European explorers came to the Americas they reported having found a new world. Columbus called Haiti "Paradise." The designation "New World" has been handed down so that it is still current usage. In what sense was or is it a new world? It certainly was not new by creation. It had been there as long as any of the great landmasses on the globe. It certainly was not new to population. The European mariners found the New World fully inhabited by peoples whose civilization, in some aspects, eclipsed that of the lands from which the explorers came. Anthropologists and archeologists are still uncovering the remnants of cultures far more advanced than that produced by what some Europeans call "primitive savages." They found pyramids in Mexico and temples of worship spread throughout the South American continent, for example. They found granaries and gold refining in areas of North America. Some of the methods of the native peoples have been adopted and transplanted to the European culture.

The New World was new because it had thitherto been unknown to these Europeans. To them here was something new indeed. It was, as it were, "The Promised Land." For our purpose I submit that it was in the Providence of God that this vast land area across forbidding seas on either side should be "discovered" when it was, by Europeans. God had reserved this New World for discovery precisely when and as it took place. America was destined to become the home of Christian culture. It is to me a marvel that, of all the religious faiths of the world, only Christianity has flourished on both the entire American continents.

From this vast reservoir of Christian strength the rest of the non-Christian world was to be exposed to the witness of the gospel and brought to the feet of Jesus. Is it any wonder that the great Christian missionary thrusts in these last days emanate from America? This is the essential task of America the Beautiful. It is the reason God has blessed it so. And this is the reason that Communism cannot succeed in America. He (God) has brought two whole continents through two world-engulfing wars with no tangible scars of destruction from either. He has blessed both great nations of North America, Canada and the United States, with humane and democratic governments. He has supplied the genius and provided the resources for the development of science and industrial technology beyond that of any other place in the world. Indeed, Daniel's prophecy that in the end time "many shall run to and fro and knowledge shall be increased" reaches its veritable fulfillment in America to a maximum degree. In the Providence of God, America is a land of spiritual destiny. Like Israel of old, with the knowledge of Jehovah to be taken to the Gentile nations, America, with the knowledge of Jesus Christ, is commissioned to spread the good news of the gospel of deliverance and PEACE to the utmost part of the earth, preparing the way of the Lord. The real national anthem of the United States of America is AMERICA.

O beautiful for spacious skies, for amber waves of grain,
For purple mountain majesties, above the fruited plain!
America! America! God shed His grace on thee
And crown thy good with brotherhood from sea to shining sea!

O beautiful for pilgrim feet, whose stern impassioned stress
A thoroughfare for freedom beat across the wilderness!
America! America! God mend thine every flaw,
Confirm thy soul in self-control, thy liberty in law!

O beautiful for heroes proved in liberating strife,
Who more than self their country loved, and mercy more than life!
America! America! may God thy gold refine,
Till all success be nobleness, and every gain divine!

O beautiful for patriot dream that sees beyond the years
Thine alabaster cities gleam undimmed by human tears!
America! America! God shed His grace on thee,
And crown thy good with brotherhood from sea to shining sea!

Katharine Lee Bates

The strains of "the rockets' red glare" and "the bombs bursting in air" ill fit this great Christian democracy. The eagle, a bird of prey, is not the true national emblem of the U.S.A. Its true national symbol is the dove, gentle harbinger of the Holy Spirit. Some day it will replace the predatory eagle, and someday the U.S.A. will adopt its proper national anthem and pursue its rightful purpose as "one nation, under God, with liberty AND JUSTICE for ALL." The black horse rider's scale will be perfectly balanced at last.

And now, I come to the crowning factor — the culminating feature — of this whole revelation: The city of God, the city foursquare. Just as the New World was already inhabited before it was discovered by the people of destiny, in like manner the city of God will be discovered and taken over by the right people and transformed into what God intended she should be.

But what is this city of destiny in the New World? IT IS WASHINGTON, DISTRICT OF COLUMBIA, capital of the United States of America. This is not my emotions effervescing. Nor is it my patriotism askew. Except by a special revelation from God, I had not known this of a certainty. More than a dozen years ago, while I was studying the Revelation in the Bible, the Lord blessed me with a depth of understanding of John's vision (of the last days of human history) which I had never reached before through many years of study. The things I shall shortly bring out are part of that knowledge.

I kept it to myself this long waiting to see if someone else, so blessed, would reveal the secret knowledge. A couple of months ago, (summer, 1980) the Lord directed me to write the vision plainly for all to read (and heed). I was told that it was for this purpose He had given it (the knowledge) to ME. This was MY assignment, MY contribution. Like the prophets of old, I had been given a special message to declare, and I would be confounded if I resisted or hesitated any longer. Like Amos, the humble shepherd of Tekoa, the "nobody" going about his business, I was waiting for other more gifted ones to sound forth the message of the hour. Also like Amos I echo him, "The lion had roared, who will not fear? The Lord God hath spoken, who can but prophesy?" It is with the deepest humility that I undertake the task.

Let us begin with the peculiarity that Washington, D.C.

is not in any of the states. This fact alone is striking. With as many as forty-eight (now fifty) states, why should this one city stand alone? Incidentally, the real number of states that conform to God's pattern is forty-eight, not fifty. The Divine design for it is the perfect square with twelve to each side, totaling forty-eight. These are all connected in the continental U.S.A. The number twelve is very important in the spiritual economy. The number of letters in "United States" totals twelve. The number in "United States of America" totals twenty-one (three sevens: 777). Seven is God's number of perfection. The letters in "America" total seven. The name of the river that runs through the nation's capitol "Potomac" has a total of seven letters. The states of Hawaii and Alaska were added to the U.S.A. for primarily military and politically strategic reasons, but they are not in God's design for the U.S.A., all the states of which are fitted together in a beautiful pattern. Interesting: each has six letters—the number of man, not God. Hawaii has already gotten the U.S.A. in serious trouble: Pearl Harbor precipitating its entrance into World War Two; Alaska will get us into serious trouble later with Russia.

But let me get back to the subject of the beloved city, Washington. The names of cities, in many cases, are indicators of their origin or meaning. Hence, Lumber City, Cedar Grove, Cedar Rapids, Mountain View, etc. Then there are names of cities that are compounded of two words that help to bring out their significance: Buena Vista, Dusty Roads, Cattle Run, Carp Lake, etc. In the case of cities that end with "ton," the ton is usually an abbreviated form of town. Thus Franklinton is really Franklin's town, Johnston is John's town, etc. Washington is such a two word combination: Town of Washing. Washing is cleansing. So Washington is literally "town (or city) of cleansing." The fact that the city bears the name of the first President, George Washington, does not change its meaning. In God's Providence what is "coincidence"? It is only a means of underscoring what God has wrought. Washington is destined to be the town of cleansing for America first and then the world, both of which need laundering spiritually and environmentally. She (Washington) is destined to be the great center in the New World to which the nations look for guidance and wisdom. She is destined to be the pacesetter, the way-shower in things that pertain to human and spiritual rectitude.

The Chief Executive of the nation is domiciled and provided working facilities in THE WHITE HOUSE, in the TOWN OF CLEANSING. Another "coincidence." The White House bears that name because of its functional relationship. It represents the highest standard of purity — of truth, righteousness, justice, compassion, peace. The designation of it as white is no more accidental than that of the horses in Revelation, chapter six. It is the very heart (life essence) of the town of cleansing. Like the temple in the midst of Israel, and the "Holy of Holies" within the temple, so the White House sits in the town of cleansing. Of course, it becomes necessary to be vigilant lest the sacred function should be prostituted. The United States was never destined to become an empire builder, but a succorer of the disadvantaged peoples of the earth. The Statue of Liberty stands as a silent proclamation of this function. The inscription it bears forever will hold out its challenge to the U.S.A.: "Give me your tired, your poor, your huddled masses yearning to breathe free, the wretched refuse of your teeming shore, send these, the homeless, tempest-tossed, to me: I lift my lamp beside the golden door." By Emma Lazarus. When an attempt was made to remodel the office of the presidency and the White House in line with an imperial motif, there was an (Watergate) eruption which, like a boil in the flesh, spewed out the festering corruption in order that a state of good health might be restored. So was it in the city of Jerusalem in a bygone day: "How is the faithful city become an harlot! It was full of judgment (justice), righteousness lodged (had its residence) in it; now murderers. Thy silver is become dross, thy wine mixed with water, Thy princes (government officials) are rebellious, and companions of thieves: everyone loveth gifts, and followeth after (is influenced by) rewards (bribes): They judge not (do not mete out justice for) the fatherless, neither doth the cause of the widow come unto them (is regarded as important to them)" (Isaiah 1:21-23). The poor and the disadvantaged were rejected in the shuffle for self-aggrandizement. So God raised up (true) prophets to call the administrators of HIS AFFAIRS back to their real responsibilities.

So was it also in the case of the temple. Jesus, The Prince of Prophets, went into the temple of Jerusalem and declared, "Is it not written, My house shall be called of all nations the house of prayer? but ye have made it a den (hideout) of thieves" (St. Mark 11:17). Mine is the voice of the latter-day prophet crying out to Washington and the White House to come back to the true destiny of preparing the peoples for the coming of the Lord, Jesus Christ because . . . .

BECAUSE HE IS COMING TO WASHINGTON! No, that is not a typographical error — or any other kind. It is according to God's revelation. Washington is (in) the District of Columbia. Columbia derives its name from Christopher Columbus, discoverer of America in the New World. The person for whom the District of Columbia is named is himself named after Christ: Christ(opher). The coming to America of Christopher Columbus symbolizes (actually heralds) the coming of Christ to His land. The District of "Christopher Columbus" is Christ's District, His headquarters. D. C. is for Dominus Christus (Lord Christ).

Now where is this district situated? We have already noted that it is not IN any state of the Union. It is situated between two states – in the middle of a two-state combination. What are they? These two states so fortunate to have this town of cleansing, this city of destiny, this city of Christ's headquarters, are Maryland and Virginia. Again, let us analyze the names of these so strategically situated states. They, too, are located there in the Providence of God and not by accidental or coincidental circumstance. Maryland is "Mary's land," literally. And Virginia is "the Virgin," again, literally. So the two states portray the Virgin Mary, the mother of Jesus, the Christ. So Washington, in the District of Columbia, is nestled in the womb of the Virgin Mary. What symbolism could be more beautiful? Or meaningful? God has written into the very geography of the planet His revelation of His Providence: "For the invisible things of him from the creation of the world are clearly seen, being understood by the things that are made, even his eternal power and Godhead; so that they are without excuse" (Rom. 1:20). In a great uranograph God has delivered His blueprint for the New Age. What "eye hath not seen, nor ear heard, neither have entered into the heart of man. . . ." God hath revealed them unto us by His Spirit: for the Spirit searcheth all things, yea, the deep things of God" (I Cor. 2:10).

So Christ emerges from the womb of the Virgin Mary and establishes His headquarters in the New World and rules. We are told in the Romans' passage quoted above that when God writes his design into the very geography of the people "they are without excuse." I reaffirm to the people who are in charge of the government of the United States of America: You are henceforth without excuse if you should let these things slip. For whether you hear me or whether you forbear, you shall yet know that a (true) prophet has been among you.

Washington is the reflected shadow of the New Jerusalem of Revelation, chapter twenty-one. It is said there that "the city lieth foursquare, and the length is as large as the breadth: and he measured the city with the reed, twelve thousand furlongs. The length and the breadth and the height of it are equal" (V. 16). When I first came to Washington the city was wholly north of the Potomac River. There were a few spill-over offices of the Federal Government in Virginia. I lived in Washington eight years and that situation changed little. However, when I received the mandate to go to Washington and write down the revelation I had received, I was astounded when, checking an ordinary road map, I saw Washington delineated as a perfect square. I could hardly believe my eyes. I took the map and traced out in bold red lines those found there by the map maker. The Federal Government has expanded to such proportions that much of its facilities are now housed across the Potomac in Virginia. So that in the midst of the city the river runs right through it, no longer bordering it to the south. I thought of the river in the city of God in Revelation: "And he showed me a pure river of water of life, clear as crystal, proceeding out of the throne of God and of the Lamb. In the midst of the street of it, and on either side of the river, was there the tree of life, which bare twelve manner of fruits, and yielded her fruit each month: and the leaves of the tree were for the healing of the nations" (Rev. 22:1-2). Never worry about the state of pollution of the present river. It will be purified.

In the description of the city in Revelation, there is an added dimension which makes it uniquely different from all earthly cities: that of HEIGHT. Who ever thought of a city having height? Yet this vertical dimension is equal to the lateral dimensions of length and breadth in the Holy City of God. You see, this SPIRITUAL city is not subject to gravitational considerations. Therefore it will have divinely-appointed installations suspended in space. There will be no problem, just as there was none for the astronauts once they were beyond the gravitational field. Never forget that the Builder and Designer of this city is God. Men who have built cities have been but inadequately tracing out in the sands of earth what they dimly observed God doing in the distant sky above them. It is easy for me to realize. I still have some relics of my son's very imperfect imitations of what he observed me doing as a carpenter when he would come around as a small child.

So the city foursquare is really a perfect cube. The square is a symbol of justice, of perfect BALANCE. Hence the familiar terms "a square deal," "fair and square," "square things up," etc. Now the relevance of the balance in the hand of the rider of the black horse may be clearly seen. He is to square things in anticipation of the coming of the city of habitation for God's people where all things will be in perpetual perfect balance.

Let me make mention of one of the buildings in the present city of Washington. Like the White House it has special significance. I refer to the Pentagon, one of America's architectural showpieces. The "penta" means "five," of course. The pentagon is the building modeled after the five-pointed Christian star in contradistinction to the six-pointed (Jewish) star of David. Since Washington is Christ's (the Christian's) headquarters, it is most appropriate that the Pentagon should be in it. The Pentagon is the largest government building in the world under one roof. It now houses the Department of Defense and serves a military function.

However, it symbolizes the facility which, in the New Age, will house a Christian Administration. There are five major world religions: Hindu, Buddhist, Judaism, Christianity, and Islam. The Pentagon dramatizes this. But the Pentagon is in Christ's Headquarters, signifying the truth that at the last "at the name of Jesus every knee should bow... and that every tongue should confess that JESUS CHRIST IS LORD to the glory of God the Father" (Phil. 2:10-11).

The old Jerusalem carries the seed of the new. The New Jerusalem will blossom (spiritually) from the stem of the old in fulfillment of the old (Testament) dispensation. The word "Jerusalem" has the location of the new in its midst: Jer-USA-lem. The USA is central. That, in the Providence of God, is because the New Jerusalem will be in the United States of America. It will be on the site of what is now Washington, D.C. Its proportions will be expanded. The New Jerusalem is for the New World. As Jesus came forth from Israel "in the fullness of time" to fulfill her spiritual destiny, so will the New Jerusalem in the New World fulfill the spiritual destiny of the old Jerusalem. Old Jerusalem is the "city of David"; the New Jerusalem is the "CITY OF GOD." Old Jerusalem is for the Jews; New Jerusalem is for the Christians. But why this distinction? Let us see.

There are two covenants involved. The old covenant is between God (Jehovah) and Israel. The New Covenant (testament) is between God and the church. Both were sealed in blood: the old, with the blood of animal, the new with the blood of Jesus, the Lamb of God without spot or blemish (of sin). Israel is the wife of Jehovah, the Father, the church is the bride of Christ, the Son of the Father.

The purpose of the Millennium is to provide for God to fulfill His promises to Israel. That is why it is of limited (1,000 years) duration. God's promises to the fathers in Israel will be fulfilled during the millennial rule of Jesus Christ, "the root and offspring of David" (Rev. 22:16). The Messiah is a Davidic Monarch in an earthly sense. The millennial kingdom will be an earthly kingdom. All natural processes will operate. People will be born, will die (a physical death only), will eat and drink, will pursue human occupations (to fill human needs); the natural seasons will make agriculture flourish, etc. People will have bodies of flesh and blood.

There will be one marked difference between life now and what it will be during the millennium THERE WILL BE NO SIN, NO EVIL. The devil and his host of demons will be locked up in the bottomless pit and therefore there will be NO TEMPTATION to sin. There will be human error, but no sin. There is a tremendous difference. God permits errors in human affairs as a means of teaching them. We grow in knowledge as we correct errors. But sin is not a mistake. Sin involves the motivation—the intentions. One may stub his toe and fall and get bruised or broken. But that does not mean he has sinned. He will certainly learn something from the experience. One sins when pursuing a course of thought and/or action he has been made aware is forbidden. "Sin is not imputed where there is no law (standard)" Rom. 5:13). One also sins whenever he fails to obey what he has been made aware is an obligation.

The people living during the millennium will be taught the ways of God as opposed to natural ways. Jesus Christ will be on the throne as Israel's recognized and accepted Ruler, the Messiah. "Out of Zion shall go forth the Law, and the word of God from (old) Jerusalem" (Isaiah 2:3). There will be a variety of kindreds and nations just as there are now. The seat of government of the whole world, however, will be Jerusalem. The once persecuted and despised Jew will be venerated and will enjoy a special place of honor. Israel shall have "received of the Lord's hand double for all her sins" (Is. 40: 2). Her iniquity will have been purged away forever by the blood of the One she crucified but now owns and obeys. She will be a faithful wife to Jehovah, her Lord.

All this will come to an end after a thousand years. The millennium is a stage, a phase in the grand unfoldment of God's Providence. It is NOT THE FINAL stage; it is NOT PERMANENT. It could no more be permanent than the old covenant under Moses could have been permanent without the coming of Jesus as Messiah to fulfill it. The perfect earthly kingdom will be a preparation for and type of the perfect spiritual kingdom which is to follow. The millennial kingdom is for the benefit of the Jew—of Israel.

Then what does the millennial kingdom have for the Christian? MUCH! The Christians, who will have been removed from the earth at the time of the rupture, will live again (upon the earth) and reign (rule) with Christ for the thousand years. They will be His deputy administrators (Rev. 5:9-10). Having suffered with Him, they will also reign with Him (II Tim. 2:12). They will be in their glorified (spiritual) bodies but will be able to assume bodies of flesh whenever necessary to carry out specific assignments. They will be "kings and priests unto God" (Rev. 1:6), ministering to Israelites, who will have no human priesthood (which was rendered obsolete), done away when Jesus Christ once offered up the perfect sacrifice, HIMSELF, on Calvary for the sins of the whole world. The Christians will be schooling the Jews (now neophyte Christians) in the ways of worshipping God not through sacrifices and rituals but from the heart through the Spirit. The true circumcision of the old covenant will find itself fulfilled. Grace must follow law in the practical affairs of the Jew. This will be for him a radical adjustment. The weight of the tradition of many centuries will roll away and the NEW ISRAELITE will come into a glorious new sense of freedom — the freedom of those whom the Son has made free (John 8:36). The Christians will have their task cut out for them and will be very busy indeed during the millennium.

We have said that the millennium comes to an end. Then what? There will occur a great shift. The days of the earthly kingdom (and ALL THINGS EARTHLY) will come to an end, including old Jerusalem, a man-made city. Jesus will deliver up the kingdom to His Father and will become subject unto Him (God's rule) who hath put all things under Him (Jesus) that God may be all in all (I Cor. 15:24-28). There will be no more physical cycles (the last enemy, being physical death, will be abolished). God's everlasting (not limited) kingdom will dawn. This will be an entirely spiritual kingdom in a New (spiritual) Age. Unlike the millennium, "there shall be no more death, neither sorrow, nor crying, neither shall there be any more pain: for the former things are passed away. And he that sat upon the throne said, Behold, I make all things new" (Rev. 21:4-5). "God Himself shall be with them and be their God." All will have permanent glorified bodies. The distinction between Christian and Jew will not exist. All will honor Christ and serve, like Christ, God the Father. The will of the Father will be everyone's only preoccupation. In this kingdom both the covenants — of law and grace — will be fulfilled. Indeed, God's purpose for the whole creation which will have been "groaning and travailing" until then waiting for the redemption (fulfillment), will be accomplished. This is that state of which the poet penned a paean when, like Abraham of old, he saw it in the distance and in his soul reached out "and embraced it": "One Lord, one faith, one element, and one far-off divine event to which the whole creation moves."

Some consideration should be given to the relationship between the two nations, Israel and the United States of America, and between the two Jerusalems, the old and the new. As Judaism and Christianity are inseparably linked, historically and spiritually, so Israel and the U.S.A. are yoked. There will never be a condition nor combination of nations able to break the bond between Israel and the U.S.A. — between Jerusalem and Washington. They are joined in the Providence of God and are therefore in an indissoluble relationship. We might term it "The Jerusalem-Washington Axis." The most visible aspect is, of course, political. But the invisible ties are stronger. Before the millennium the political bond will be primary. During the millennium it will be essentially a spiritual relationship, although the economic and political aspects will be manifest. Before the millennium there will be military alignment in facing a common foe. During the millennium there will be no military establishment, for "the earth shall be filled with the knowledge of the glory of the Lord as the waters cover the sea" (Hab. 2:14). "And they shall beat their swords into plowshares, and their spears into pruning hooks: nation shall not lift up sword against nation, neither shall they learn war (study military science and tactics) anymore" (Ia. 2:4).

Old Jerusalem being man-made, is destined to pass away. New Jerusalem will never pass away. It cannot. It is the promise of God to the children of Abraham BY FAITH, that they should "enter into HIS REST." Now it is said (Hebrews 11:10) of Abraham "for he looked for a city which hath foundations, whose builder and Maker is God." It is further stated of Abraham and those sharing his faith and the promises made by God to him: "But now they desire a better country, that is, an heavenly : Wherefore God is not ashamed to be called their God: For HE hath PREPARED for them a city" (Heb. 11:16). The "them" are the children of Abraham BY FAITH, i.e., Christians. When a Jew manifests the faith of Abraham, he professes faith in Jesus Christ as Savior, and in so doing, is no longer a Jew but a Christian (Christ-redeemed one), no longer expecting his sins to be atoned for by the blood of sacrificial animals, and no longer expecting to be justified by the works of the Law of Moses.

In Revelation (Chapter 21), like Daniel's stone hewed out of the mountain without (human) hands, the holy city, New Jerusalem, comes down from God PREpared. John saw it "descending" from God out of the heavens complete in every detail. Man, i.e., the redeemed of the Lord Jesus Christ, can only inhabit it. This, like salvation, is a gift from his Maker, the heritage of the redeemed of the Lord. In Revelation 15: 13 there is described a group of saints standing on a sea of glass in heaven. It is called a "sign" in heaven, "great and marvellous." "And I saw as it were a sea of glass mingled with fire: and them that had gotten the victory over the beast, and over his image, and over his mark, and over the number of his name, stand on the sea of glass, having the harps of God. And they sing the song of Moses the servant of God, AND the song of the Lamb, saying, Great and marvellous are thy works, Lord God Almighty; just and true are thy ways thou King of saints." This is something new for the Israelite. They could sing only the song of Moses before they were redeemed by the blood of the Lamb, Jesus Christ. Now they are able to sing both (as were the Christians all the time). "There shall be one fold and one shepherd" (St. John 10:16). All the redeemed of the Lord shall hear (heed) His voice. They are led by Him to fountains of living (life-giving) water. "They shall hunger no more, neither thirst any more; neither shall the sun light on them, nor any heat. For the Lamb which is in the midst of the throne shall feed them, and shall lead them unto living fountains of waters: and God shall wipe away all tears from their eyes" (Rev. 7:16-17). This is the true consummation of the Age, the fulfillment of the destiny of the world. It will come to pass as surely as yesterday has passed. To those who look with longing for its dawning, take hope. "Be patient therefore, brethren, unto the coming of the Lord; for the coming of the Lord draweth nigh" (James 5:8). To those who are "fearful, and unbelieving, and the abominable, and murderers, and whoremongers, and sorcerers, and idolaters, and all liars" (Rev. 21:8), "Repent ye, and believe the gospel" (St. Mark 1:15).

Chapter Seven

THE CONCLUSION OF THE WHOLE MATTER

I have said all this to say what? What conclusions are we to draw from the data here presented? What lessons can we learn that will help to prepare us for what we have a chance to see unfolding and in which we are inextricably involved?

First, the events of human history, indeed all phenomena, are by the direction and under the surveillance of a Divine Providence — Almighty God. This God is a Person, not an impersonal force. He conceives, wills, projects, purposes, proposes and disposes according to His sovereign will. The plan of God is beautifully designed and meaningful in every detail. This whole universe, of which our earth is but a microscopic speck, is not a happenstance or chance affair, but truly: "The heavens declare the glory of God, and the firmament showeth His handiwork" (Ps. 19:1).

Second, the God of the universe is good: kind, loving, benevolent. He is no ruthless, uncaring monster. Nor is He indifferent. The very word "good" is the same as "God" with one letter omitted, and is derived from it. Any other way of perceiving this marvellous universe and its relationship to God is a perversion of thought, a distortion of perspective. "All things work together for good to them that love God, to them who are the called according to His purpose" (Rom. 8:28).

Third, in the ongoing process of the unfolding of God's grand design, nothing is permanent but God Himself, and, from Him, His word. God's word is the projection of His Mind and will and therefore is inexorable and eternal: "The grass withereth, the flower fadeth: but the word of our God shall stand forever" (Ia. 40:8). "Forever, O Lord, thy word is settled in heaven" (Ps. 119:89). "Heaven and earth shall pass away, but my words shall not pass away" (Mat. 24:35).

Fourth, in this constantly fluctuating panorama we call history, different peoples at different times, their cultures (with all the diverse components thereof) rise and fall, proceed, halt, and recede as God who called them forth, equipped them, gave them license, directs. It is He who raises up one and puts down another as it suits His purpose. The human ego is the most hazardous of man's hurdles — the most formidable of his foes — because it tends to blind him to the very One who gave man his role and who is directing the drama. The human ego promotes the feeling: "By my own cunning (genius) have I contrived this and by the strength of my right arm have I accomplished it." I can remember vividly that when one of my children was but a few years old, I would sit her in my lap and let her (at her request) "drive the car." Of course I knew better, but she didn't. Her hands were on the steering wheel, but so were my stronger, longer ones. And further, my foot was at the accelerator and the brake, neither of which her feet could reach.

Fifth, in these last years of human history — its closing phase — the principal character in the last act is identifiable with the black race. The rider of the black horse in Revelation has been held in the wings for this hour. Now he is sent forth to play his part. Nothing will hinder him. Africans (and Afro-Americans) have a special place of exaltation and responsibility among the nations and in the beloved city. Africans have suffered most among the nations and yet have remained humble and patient. Afro-Americans have suffered most in the new world and yet have kept faith in the Christian gospel and Christian democracy. That is why the blacks now hold the BALANCE of power in the United Nations. That is why the blacks (Black Caucus) wield a powerful influence in the Congress of the United States of America. That is why the blacks were the BALANCE of power in the presidential election of 1976 that succeeded in getting a southern (Georgia) farmer in the White House. That is why the blacks, who for generations were systematically and categorically excluded from professional sports, now dominate many of them. Consider what Henry Aaron has done to Babe Ruth's home run record, what Muhammed Ali has done for the boxing arena—the greatest overall record in history. Even in soccer, a sport which until recently nobody associated with blacks, Edson A. N. Pele, a black, has distinguished himself as the greatest in the game. Basketball's and football's Hall of Fame are beginning to get top-heavy with black scions. These are only a few, cited to clinch the point. Some of America's greatest cities are becoming accustomed to black mayorial administrations. The capitol of the U.S.A., Washington, D.C., since becoming self-governing, has had only black mayors. Washington has had a predominantly black population for generations and is increasing in black political control. This is an anomaly in view of the fact that the United States of America has always been an overwhelmingly, predominantly white nation at the top of a white civilization. I predict that a black president is destined to occupy the White House.

Sixth, the cleanup of Washington spiritually, morally, and physically is the special God-given task of the blacks. It will be accomplished by black initiative, although other minorities will play a significant part. Washington will be the pacesetter for America in general. The speed with which this will be done will astound many.

Let it not be misconstrued: what I have set forth in this treatise. My purpose is not to discredit the white race or White Christians, many of whom are giving dedicated and sacrificial service. Nor is it to promote the so-called "black cause." Neither virtue nor vice may be found to divide according to racial lines except by the circumstances of political history and the socio-economic situation. That "God is no respecter of persons" is uncontestable as far as I am concerned.

Once while musing on the many wonderful and praiseworthy things about America, a solemn thought came to my mind. As I thought of the cradle of our democracy in the New World, Philadelphia, the "city of brotherly love," the Liberty Bell loomed up before me. I saw the inscription (from my Bible) that adorns it: "Proclaim liberty throughout all the land unto all the inhabitants thereof..." (Lev. 25: 10). Then, slowly, almost imperceptibly at first, I saw the crack in the Liberty Bell. Unmistakably it was there. Why should there be this flaw in so noble a symbol? Would it be there as an ugly wound for each succeeding generation to gaze upon, wondering why the scar? I found my pen in hand, and my reflections, like snowflakes crystallizing, froze on the page before me:

THE CRACK IN THE LIBERTY BELL

There is a crack in the Liberty Bell that rang out
                                o'er the land.
There is a flaw, the sound is marred; 'tis somewhat
                                hollow-canned
When sounding forth to reassure of liberty for all,
Regardless of our race or creed, be we of great or small.

The bell became a souvenir, much prized but set aside.
To gaze upon, but not to use, for practice is denied
The very object for which need brought motive to create,
And gathering dust on top of rust became its latter state.

The fire beneath the melting pot has almost been put out;
'Tis difficult to find the side on which appears the spout
Through which the blended product flows from
                                all-and-sundry ore
Of native, alien, black and white, of wealthy and of poor.

Where once with such felicity they mingled with great ease,
Now blows a rather chilling wind with threat of icy freeze
In all of the relationships by which we gained the name
"America the Beautiful" that inspired world acclaim.

Two worldwide wars on foreign soil preserved our heritage—
Endowment with "inalienable rights" beyond the sacred page
On which was once inscribed the faith our founding fathers
                                knew,
We fought and won through sacrifice and singleness of view.

With threat of bondage to our outside foes now turned away,
Relaxed, pursued ev'ry man his solitary way.
Pursued his self-determined goal to gain his own desire
While thoughts of "general welfare" were tossed into the fire.

"More perfect union" soon became extraneous to the ear—
"Domestic tranquility" expressed much less faith than fear.
"Blessings of liberty to ourselves and our posterity"
Was now "hush-hush" among our vets and youth especially.

The sound that once around the world was heard so loud
            and clear—
The guarantees to our allies of freedom from all fear,
In ever-dimming waves and so irregular now come;
Our face abroad no longer seen as that we claim at home.

Domestic discord on that face has etched out many scars;
The statue of our liberty a foggy veil now mars.
Though still its torch 'tis lifting high within the harbor bar,
One has to draw real close to see and feel the freedom star.

No longer can its gleam be seen from far across the seas;
But very faintly now is heard our anthem on the breeze;
For there's a crack in Liberty Bell as it rings out now;
'Tis caused by all the hate and strife that you and I allow.

A souvenir is beautiful when mounted on the wall;
Our Liberty Bell is picturesque in Independence Hall;
But there are times when crucial and when dire momentous
            need
Demand the use of all we have; and we the voice must heed.

This day, an humble citizen, I'm bowing deep in prayer,
When all around my feet gives way—when hope invites
despair:
"Dear God, in mercy lead us to recast our Liberty Bell—
Lift our democracy heavenward—save us once more from hell.

Send Thy Holy Spirit to bring peace, goodwill to all;
Forgive our follies manifold: uphold us, lest we fall.
Give us the courage, Lord, I pray, the crack to fully heal;
O once more let the self-same bell throughout our country
peal."
The Author — September 11, 1963, 6:30 a.m.

BLACKS WHEREVER YOU ARE, THIS IS YOUR SHINING HOUR. ASSUME YOUR RESPONSIBILITY. RISE TO THE CHALLENGE. YOUR SUN HAS RISEN. YOUR NIGHT HAS PAST. YOUR DAY HAS DAWNED. FULFILL YOUR DESTINY UNDER GOD.